The Genesis of Marxism

Four Lectures

Also for Dent by R. N. Berki

Socialism (Modern Ideologies Series), 1975
The History of Political Thought: a short introduction, 1977
On Political Realism, 1981
Insight and Vision: the problem of communism in Marx's thought, 1983
Security and Society: reflections on law, order and politics, 1986

The Genesis of Marxism

Four Lectures

R. N. Berki

Dent: London
EVERYMAN'S UNIVERSITY LIBRARY

First published 1988
© R. N. Berki, 1988

Made in Great Britain by
Butler & Tanner for
J. M. Dent & Sons Ltd
91 Clapham High Street, London SW4 7TA

British Library Cataloguing in Publication Data

Berki, R. N. (Robert Nandor), 1936–
   the genesis of Marxism : four lectures.
   1. Marxism
   I. Title
   335.4

ISBN 0-460-13000-5
ISBN 0-460-15780-9 Pbk

PREFACE

The text before the reader is based on an undergraduate course bearing the same title, offered as an option to students taking the special Hull degree, European Studies, in their final year, and to all-comers. I have run this course for three years, and before that its parent course in the Politics Department, 'Hegel and the Origins of Marxism', for some twelve years. The book is a condensation, therefore, of twenty-two formally delivered lectures and an equal number of seminar discussions, their content slowly maturing over time. It was my intention in this text to preserve as much as possible from the 'live' course, particularly its convivial atmosphere. Hence the choice of genre, viz. 'four lectures', which might seem a bit odd at first. There is no difficulty about the four-fold division which is based on thematic considerations. But perhaps I should explain why I call the four pieces 'lectures'. The length of each, obviously, far exceeds the length of a typical university lecture, orally presented. What I endeavoured to do was to recreate the flavour of the lecture, with its mixed salad menu of factual information, interpretive comment, bridging generalizations, and the occasional light-hearted aside. The lecture, it seems to me, is a distinct form of communication, irrespective of its length, which should not be confused with the 'study' or 'essay' or 'treatise'. Its essence is direct communication with a definite audience, and its primary purpose is stimulation. However, I must also make it clear that although 'introductory' in design, this is not meant to be a 'noddy' text: it addresses people (students and all-comers) who have an interest in and already understand the basic language of political and social theory. In our subject − unlike, I suppose, in maths and natural science − it is in any case impossible to write 'pure' introductions: information is inseparable from interpretation. Here, as readers will note, the interpretive aspect is pretty large and grows larger as we move on. I am fully aware that every statement made in the foregoing is open to questioning. But I would also like to believe that every statement can be defended. I hope I will be excused for dispensing with footnotes which in this exercise would have been an unnecessary pedantry. The Select Bibliography – a little bit skewed, perhaps – contains for the most part works which I myself particularly enjoyed reading and which probably influenced me most over the years.

I must express my gratitude, first of all, to generations of students who, through their written work and verbal challenges, inadvertently contributed to the content of the present work; many, as they have put it to me, 'got something out of the course'; now I have managed to get something out of them. My immense gratitude goes also to two cherished professorial friends and mentors, David McLellan of the University of Kent and Bhikhu Parekh of our own Politics Department, who took on the unrewarding chore of reading the first draft without demur, and enabled me to correct numerous mistakes. So did my colleague, Dr Peter Stirk, Leverhulme Fellow in the Department of European and Modern Dutch Studies, to whom I owe additional thanks for taking on some lectures and seminars in the same course in 1987/8 – entirely for love! But while I happily acknowledge their help, I would like to stress that in no way could these three esteemed academics be held responsible for the views presented in the text. And last but not least I am recording my heartfelt thanks to Jacky Peters, also of our Department, who did an excellent job, with deadline looming, of transcribing my honest but rough typescript on to that invention of the devil, the word-processor.

Hull, January 1988   R. N. B.

CONTENTS

CONCEPTION

There is, if you like, one big idea running through these four lectures. This idea is that Marxism belongs centrally to the mainstream tradition of European political and social theory and that therefore the most advantageous way in which to be introduced to the thought of Karl Marx – the vital centre of Marxism – is through a study of its genesis in the womb of this tradition. This is by no means an original or sensational idea. Yet it is not an empty cliché either, for I intend to take this 'traditional' character of Marxism here seriously and shall attempt, which within the confines of these lectures will of course have to be done in a rather concise manner, to present its distinctive features – peculiar excellences and shortcomings – by pointed reference to its intellectual derivation. What my interpretation will indirectly question is a popularly held view of Marx on both the political (and academic) Left and Right. It is that the essential thing about Marx's thought is its radicalism and novelty, its thoroughgoing 'revolutionary' character, opposing and contradicting the underlying values and organizing concepts of the mainstream tradition. Of course Marxism is meant to be a doctrine of social, political and intellectual revolution. Nevertheless what this popular view of the 'marketplace' tends to overlook is, firstly, that Marx stood out of the ranks of great revolutionary thinkers, in his time as well as before and after, for his 'moderation in revolution'. It was Marx who stressed the importance of ripening 'objective conditions' of revolution and he who insisted that the revolution would be succeeded by a lengthy 'transition period' before the arrival of the good society, i.e. communism. Secondly, and this is really the crucial point in our context, on examination Marxist revolutionary values and concepts will be seen squarely to reflect, not just an isolated European 'revolutionary tradition', but the

1

latent revolutionary message of the mainstream itself. Marxism is revolutionary *because* it is traditional and our great historical heritage could produce something like the doctrine and movement of Marxism in modern times *because* it has always carried the germs (or perhaps I should say 'sperms') of revolution within it.

I will assume, and in its proper place (i.e. in the fourth lecture) argue, that Marx's thought has an underlying unity which can be rendered intelligible by being presented as the achieved 'synthesis' of major perspectives and departures located in the European tradition. The 'synthesis' – conceptual gathering – is achieved but this means no more in Marx's case than a momentary and conjunctural glory which Marxism *in the world* has not be able to sustain. But Marxism 'in the world' is not our concern here (except for a few remarks later on). Marxism 'coming into' the world is. Ours will be a retrospective and historically deconstructive glance, endeavouring to build up (or reconstitute) the Marxist synthesis from its basic elements, themselves historically unfolding. Viewing Marxism as synthesis in this sense means also using it as a powerful prism through which to gain an informed glimpse of some interesting features of our inherited culture and civilization. It will be argued that the Marxist synthesis operates on two distinct, though closely interrelated, levels. In an historically more circumscribed context – that is, viewed within the confines of *modern* European thought – it represents a 'conceptual gathering' of three doctrinal departures. But on a deeper and historically more extensive level it signifies the accomplished unity of two fundamental perspectives built into European thought from its very origins; the coming together of these two perspectives is itself the essential definition of modernity.

In this first lecture I shall be mainly concerned with the 'conception' of Marx's thought, and by 'conception' I am referring simply to its broader and deeper intellectual background, in particular the two fundamental perspectives of European thought mentioned above. But even before that, a general characterization of what I am calling here the European (or 'Western') *mainstream* will be in order. It seems reasonable to suggest, as a first approximation, that European political and social thought has in the main concerned itself with the notions of 'reason', 'movement', 'struggle' and 'freedom'. With some audacity it might even be surmised that these notions express the distinct identity of Western culture as such, in contrast to others. 'Reason' refers here to the assumed ability of human beings to abstract and generalize from experience and to have experience guided by thought. It highlights the conviction that human action is most effective and satisfying when directly connected with thinking, and conversely that the human *understanding* of reality reaches its highest accolade in *action*, in making a difference to the world. By 'movement' I refer to the acceptance of infinity and change, the acknowledgment (happy or rueful as the case may be) that intellectual 'truths' as well as concrete forms of the 'good society' are subject to decay, refutation and supersession, that the flow of human history has an uncertain destination. 'Struggle' means the conviction, running through our entire culture, that human beings are constantly 'up against it', that reality has to be confronted in order that human reason – action informed by thinking – may become and remain effective. Lastly 'freedom', the most intriguing, most distinctive but at the same time most difficult concept of the European tradition: it signifies above all the positive value attached to the very *uncertainties* accompanying the human confrontation with reality, the joys and tribulations involved in thinking and acting, the struggle to remove the barriers to soaring human thought and determined action, to achieve the mastery of self and external reality, to enlarge human space and time.

It is along these lines, it seems to me, that a useful distinction could be drawn between the Western tradition and those with which it has come into historical contact. To attempt to draw these large distinctions is of course an exercise fraught with danger but (for this very reason) it is also fascinating; besides, such a distinction is quite relevant to the unfolding argument of these lectures. I think it would be by and large true to say that what the 'West' has found in the 'East' (China and India for example), from Herodotos to Montesquieu to R. D. Laing, is the very opposite of the four notions mentioned above. As against Western reason here there has been emphasis on internal

3

spirituality and transcending the world by turning away from it; as against movement there has been a sense of permanent order and the 'eternal return'; as against confrontation and struggle an attitude of reverence towards external reality and the desire to be united with it; as against assertive freedom and the love of uncertainty willing acquiescence in the wheel of everlasting necessity. Obviously I am simplifying matters to some extent. We should be clear, at any rate, about two things. Firstly the erection of large and abstract models, like Western and Eastern culture, must always go with the recognition that they have never been completely divorced from each other but have developed through constant and mutual cross-fertilization (especially conspicuous in our own times, the closing decades of the twentieth century). Secondly there is no way – as far as I can see, at any rate – in which to establish the 'superiority' of either East or West by reference to these or any other concepts and values. These great traditions are *there*, with their own distinctive identity, their own internal validity and coherence, their peculiar wisdom as well as their more doubtful features. The endeavour of these lectures is confined to the making of a few (sensible or otherwise) *historical* judgments, with the purpose of facilitating an understanding of the genesis of Marxism; I am not consciously interested in making here any judgments of value. And this may be the opportune moment to make it entirely clear that Marxism is also viewed in these lectures as something *there*, as an effective intellectual and political force in the contemporary world. Whether or not it is a force for 'the good' is not our concern; people have to make up their own mind about that. However, what I *am* arguing in these lectures is that value-judgments of this sort are best based on a proper understanding of the thing to be judged, and that in the case of Marxism an appreciation of its genesis – its conception, gestation, formation and fruition in the European mainstream – is (at the very minimum) an integral part of this understanding.

At this point I should offer an initial, working definition of Marxism, as viewed in these lectures. In the light of what I have just now highlighted as the four predominant notions in the European mainstream tradition of political and social theory, I propose that we look upon Marxism primarily as a doctrine of *human liberation* where 'liberation' or 'freedom' is understood in this distinctive Western sense of rational mastery of the self and external reality. It will be convenient here, further, to define Marx's thought initially as a doctrine of human liberation taking place (or rather, envisaged and intended to take place) in three dimensions simultaneously. In the first place, liberation occurs in the relationship between human beings and *nature*: freedom here is the full realization of human reason in the external world, the understanding of human potential and the limits of natural necessity, and the ordering of human affairs accordingly. Secondly, liberation takes place in the realm of human *society*. This is of course the most conspicuous aspect of Marxist doctrine, being above all a specimen of the genre 'political and social theory'. But as students of Marx we would neglect the other two dimensions at our peril! The liberation of society – which in Marxist thought signifies also the liberation of human individuals in and for society – means above all the elimination of conflict between determinate social groups, 'classes' in the modern age, and the ending of oppression and exploitation of some groups by others. Marxism looks forward, in the distant but foreseeable and realizable future, to the 'communist' society of freely thinking and acting, rational, productive, happy and 'social' individuals. This will arrive after the victorious revolution of the 'toilers of the world' and will signify the beginning of *human* history in the proper sense. The third dimension of human liberation in Marxist thought is the liberation of the *mind*. This is perhaps the most difficult to understand – or easiest to underrate – but for Marx it is the lynchpin of the whole process of liberation, the intellectual foundation and presupposition of the other two dimensions as well as their triumphant culmination. The essence of this is the full understanding – nay, conscious experience – of the moral freedom and self-sufficiency of the human species, i.e. the understanding that the rational human being is *as such* free, self-creating and self-determining in natural and social relationships, recognizing no alien moral superior in the entire universe. To put it another way, we might say that the communist perspective in Marx's doctrine involves, or breaks down into, the three interrelated elements of *social science* (i.e. knowledge and mastery of nature), *socialism* and *humanism*.

Now, having initially defined Marxism this way, as a *three-pronged* doctrine of human liberation, we may immediately proceed on to noticing the three major and influential departures in modern European thought of which Marxist doctrine has conventionally been regarded as the 'synthesis'. The reason why I proceeded this way: from an initial definition of Marxism back to Marx's predecessors, was to bring home the truth that these elements which Marx is said to have received from his predecessors, and adapted so as to produce his own elaborate perspective, are indeed *internal* to Marxism, that the very character, very essence, very unity of Marx's doctrine is that it is 'synthetic'. In a most dramatic sense: the meaning of Marxism is the genesis of Marxism is the synthesis achieved and embodied in Marxism. (A sentence which I shall paraphrase, and explain more fully, in the concluding lecture.)

Well then, what is it precisely that Marxism is the synthesis of? Obviously, as every student would know, it is the synthesis of English political economy, French radical socialism, and German idealist philosophy. Marx himself in numerous indirect references, and Engels and Lenin quite explicitly, acknowledged that these three departures had supplied the foundations of what became Marxist doctrine. I can see no overwhelming reason why Marx's own understanding of his intellectual background, and Marxist conventional wisdom following him, should not be accepted at more or less their face value. Indeed, I am taking this conventional view as my departure and shall endeavour, in the sequel, only to enrich its content and highlight its significance. It will thus be taken for granted that in the main Marx's social science, his socialism and his humanism do derive respectively from the writings of English classical political economists, the communist and utopian socialist thinkers of France, and Hegel and his leftwing disciples in Germany; Marxism does speak, predominantly, the 'language' of these three great modern traditions.

Marx as a matter of fact never claimed originality except for certain restricted (though significant) parts of his doctrine, and regarded his own achievement consciously as one of a synthesizer, one who had dotted the i's and crossed the t's, who had drawn clear and emphatic conclusions from the premises of his intellectual mentors. The most famous example, of course, is the claim made in the Preface to the first volume of *Capital*, concerning the Hegelian dialectic, the 'rational kernel' of which is supposed to have been incorporated in Marx's science of political economy, and turned back from its head on to its feet. Perhaps we should briefly add here – so as to get a more balanced picture of Marx's own appraisal of the aforementioned three departures – that Marx's acknowledgment of his various intellectual debts alas did not preclude his treating his immediate predecessors and likeminded contemporaries with ridicule and heavy paternalism, and often with contempt and venom. This in spite of the fact that he tended to ascribe the superiority of his own perspective to those of the economists, philosophers and political thinkers not to his personal genius but to his historical vantage-point (somewhat like a preacher claiming to be God's humble mouth-piece).

But back to these three modern 'sources' of Marxism. While they are undoubtedly *there*, and undoubtedly 'internal' to Marxist doctrine, supplying the content and language of Marx's three-dimensional theory of human liberation, it will still not do to stop with them and attempt to account for the genesis of Marxism simply on their level. There are several reasons why it is advisable (indeed *necessary*) to dig even further into the 'deep foundations', to what is being designated here as the *conception* of Marxist doctrine in the historical background of our entire tradition, and although these lectures primarily serve an introductory purpose it is important for us to note them here, at least summarily. In the first place, Marx himself was conscious of having learnt from many other sources, besides political economy, socialist theory and practice, and humanist philosophy: from life itself around him, from the reality of capitalism in England, from the famous Blue Books, from all kinds of literary, philosophical, religious and scientific texts, ancient and modern, etc. In the second place, and more relevantly in the context, note should be taken of the fact that these three alleged main 'sources' of Marxism do not – except in a rather superficial historical gaze, not permissible even in an introduction of this kind and brevity – stand neatly to attention as clearly identifiable, mutually isolated and successively surfacing 'chunks' in the history of ideas. In truth these separate sources are more or less chronologically simultaneous in historical appearance and constantly and mutually interpenetrating and cross-fertilizing – as well as clashing. There is definitely a sort of humanist philosophy in English political economy and in French socialism, just as there is political economy embedded in the other two streams. The national tag is a convenient abbreviation in each case, nothing more. And besides there is a real and important sense in which the very *conceptualization* of these three modern departures as the 'sources' of Marxism is wholly *retrospective* and thus – as the guardians of a pure and proper 'history of ideas' will tell us – intellectually suspect. In Marx something called English political economy, French socialism and German philosophy do smoothly dovetail and productively complement one another; but these are not necessarily the doctrines as we find them, say, with Adam Smith, Ricardo, Babeuf and Blanqui, Saint-Simon, Hegel and Feuerbach. Still, though we have to take note of this difficulty, let us not make too much heavy weather of it: as I hope to show in subsequent lectures, there *is* a great deal indeed in the writings of these and other predecessors which does 'foreshadow' or 'prefigure' or even 'anticipate' the doctrine of Marx in a significant and interesting way.

It is, however, the third reason which personally I find most telling here, albeit it is also the simplest. Let us assume, for the sake of argument and convenience, that Marxism is essentially built on these three foundations and that these foundations are historically 'there', being proper objects of study. It is still not only pertinent but absolutely vital (as well as being absolutely fascinating) to go on to ask further questions: *why* are they there in the first place? Where do they come from? It will be seen at once that any enterprise which leads us from a study of Marxism to the study of the genesis of Marxism will be taking us even further than the level of these immediate modern predecessors. On the one hand it is certainly legitimate and reasonable to surmise that the 'originality' of Marx's intellectual forebears was not of a higher order than Marx's own; as Marx learnt, so had they; as Marx drew explicit conclusions from half-hidden premises, so had they. And on the other hand the very perception of historical 'transmission' in this restricted context (Marxism and its three modern sources) should make us generally more attentive to transmissive sequences occurring also on a larger scale. At one point we shall have to probe the nature – origin and emergence – of that very standpoint of *modernity* which both spawned and legitimized these three departures themselves, the 'wisdom of the age' which pronounced them valid and rational and which, in the fullness of time, was to put a stamp of reasonableness on Marxism too, their ultimate offspring. As Marxism did not appear out of the blue, neither had modern political economy, socialist movements and humanist philosophy been born in an unfathomable, unintelligible vacuum. We must dig even further. The path leads, inevitably, to a consideration of our tradition as a whole, and with particular reference to those of its features which will shed some light on the emergence and nature of the modern age, together with its furthest-flung consequences (among them Marxism, which the philosopher Jean-Paul Sartre not entirely inaccurately called the 'philosophy of our epoch'). There is no denying that this is quite a bold step to take and not without some rather obvious pitfalls. However, in view of the overall design of these lectures this procedure still seems preferable to me, and it will at the least relieve us from the tedium and triviality involved in myopically tracing minute changes, from one generation to the next. The historian's nightmare of infinite regress can only be escaped if we are determined to proceed directly to the roots themselves. Indeed later on, in accordance with the demands imposed on us by the subject matter, we shall considerably sharpen our focus; but for now the main task is to get the larger contours into proper perspective.

What I am essentially arguing is that the modern outlook, with its theoretical outflowing into the three realms of philosophy, economy and social organization, is itself to be seen as a *synthesis*, in more or less the same sense as Marx's thought is capable of characterization as the synthesis of the three modern departures. Modernity has a unity of its own, to be sure, but this is still a unity of separate and identifiable elements. Modernity as a 'unity of differences' can, it seems to me – to proceed now a step further – be conveniently described in terms of our projected definition of the Marxist doctrine of human liberation, bearing in mind its (as yet hypothetical) derivation from central ideas found in the European mainstream. It will be recalled that the Marxist perspective, as we defined it, emphasized liberation in the human relationship to nature, society and the mind; in each of these three dimensions the supreme aim and value of *freedom* is connected to an achievement of human *reason*. These two, freedom and reason, are supreme and perhaps we might say perennial values in European culture and civilization, the operative terms in all departures worthy to be labelled social and political philosophy, and together with the ideas of movement and struggle (as we suggested earlier) they might be said to constitute the distinct identity of Western thought in this particular area. With a slight shift of emphasis an element of order could be introduced into this group – or collection – of ideas. *Freedom* could be seen to subsume the most important values – moral, social, political – of European culture. And *reason* could and should be elevated as the concentrated expression of the crucial role assigned to knowledge, thinking, concepts, arguments in the mainstream tradition. What we have then is a spectrum of social and political philosophy defined in terms of its two extreme 'poles' of freedom and reason, or valuation and cognition.

On this basis let us then suggest, firstly, that in Marxism there is a *visionary* element, connoting value-assumptions and ultimate aims; in concrete terms this is to be defined as freedom, happiness, the good society, communism. And in Marxism there is also a *cognitive* element, which refers to the knowledge or understanding of the world; concretely this has reference to Marx's theories of history, political economy, social classes, the state, ideology, and revolution. The Marxist vision, if you like, transcends the world of actual existence, whereas Marxist learning or Marxist 'insight' starts out from this world; it is the latter, the realm of human reason, which takes account of the 'movement' of human history and the 'struggle' going on in human society. And secondly I would like to argue that the mainstream European tradition of political and social thought is not only to be defined in terms of a spectrum connecting the two poles of freedom and reason but that – originally and analytically – it shows a *cleavage* between two fundamental perspectives. I shall postulate, in other words, that in the depth of the European tradition the perspective of vision, trans- cendence, value and the perspective of knowledge and under- standing are antithetical and divided. In the next section of this lecture I shall develop this deep-lying antithesis. In the third section I shall devote some thought to modernity, presented here as the synthesis of the two perspectives. The arrival of modernity of course, in terms of the interpretation advanced in these lectures, signifies the close of the phase of 'Conception' in the genesis of Marxism.

*   *   *   *   *

What I am calling here the two fundamental perspectives of our tradition are the crystallized result of a process of 'distillation' from a number of sources. I shall later refer directly to some of these sources but first I would like to spend some time defining the distilled perspectives themselves, in simple terms. On the one hand, then, it is argued here that European political and social theory contains a tradition of *transcendence*, a visionary, moralistic and 'softhearted' perspective which is largely the legacy of classical idealist philosophy and religion. And on the other hand our culture contains a tradition of *understanding*, a hardheaded and 'scientific' perspective which derives in the main from ancient philosophies of materialism and realism. To start with the first one, this perspective operates with a notion of a perfect, ideal world, distant from and defined in sharp contrast to 'actual existence' but one which serves as the yardstick for our comprehension of actual existence and which also supplies the motive force and justification of political action. This is of course not confined to 'revolutionary' political action (and definitely not to 'revolution' in the narrower modern, and *a fortiori* Marxist, sense) but as we shall see later the idealistic tradition can always be very easily pushed in this direction. The transcendent vision, the tradition of moral and political idealism, is a necessary *intellectual presupposition* of modern doctrines of revolution – this is the reason why I had the temerity, in the very first paragraph of this lecture, to suggest that revolutionary Marxism was 'traditional' precisely in *being* revolutionary. The tradition of transcendence is an integral part of its original 'conception'.

Taking a closer look now at this idealistic perspective, four ideas it seems to me stand out as being particularly worthy of attention in the present context. The first is the idea of the *benevolent universe*. This refers to the belief that there is somewhere and in some form a basic 'sense' or rationality in reality, a sense which human beings can come to comprehend, however dimly, and one which, if approached in the correct way, will assist them in their endeavours to reach their sundry goals and satisfy their yearnings. This benevolent universe can be defined in several ways: as a personal deity, a father, creator and lawgiver, or as an impersonal but 'ordered' reality governed by immutable and inexorable laws. The main point is that an approach by humans is possible: if we but follow the true path, by having faith or the right ideas or doing the right things, then our eventual success is assured. The universe itself more or less guarantees that efforts are not expended in vain; ultimate reality itself shows us the way in which to transcend actual existence.

The second is the idea of transcendent and objective *morality*. It is maintained in terms of this idealistic perspective that 'good' and 'evil' are built into the universe, that they are integral parts of reality, given from above or from outside or from our 'innermost being', unalterable and universal, not to be tampered with or to be defied; evil conduct will be punished by nature itself. The 'good' is broadly understood here as a cluster of qualities, or ways of life, which most closely reflect the nature of the benevolent universe itself; human beings, therefore, are to be *raised* to be worthy of their 'real' selves, irrespective of their immediate inclinations. The good is that which enhances life; evil is that which is destructive of life, which is a diminution of life, which keeps human beings shackled to *mere* actual existence and away from contact and union with the ultimate and benevolent reality shining in the distance. The triumph of good over evil is of course assured; however, evil really exists, it is a force in the world of actual existence, and has therefore to be fought against relentlessly.

The third important idea to be found in this perspective is

the *elevation of the species*. The idealistic stance firmly maintains that humanity is unique: it does contain evil, to be sure, but nevertheless among all naturally known creatures this species is alone capable of rising, of transcending its own actual existence. Humanity is the sole representative of ultimate reality, of a higher benevolent universe, of transcendent goodness, in the heterogeneous here and now. The conviction blazes right through this tradition of idealism over the centuries – from Moses to Plato to Marx – that the difference between the human species on the one hand and all other natural species is *qualitative* and fundamental: 'man' (meaning the species, not the gender), with the spark of transcendence, has alone the potential to become the 'lord of nature'. As it is with the idea of the benevolent universe, the mark of distinction attaching to the human species has been defined in many different ways: man alone is created in the image of God, humans alone have immortal souls, human beings are distinguished from animals by their ability to reason, to think, to use language, to create and maintain 'culture' over and above external nature, to apply their productive energies, led and governed by their unique rationality, to nature and transform nature in the process. This assumed uniqueness and superiority of the human race, of course, need not be – and in the fact, for the most part, has not been – understood as involving the right of tyrannical irresponsibility towards the rest of nature. On the contrary, higher being is assumed to go with a higher sense of 'duty'. But it should be noted that in this perspective the human race is seen to have responsibility *for* nature, rather than *to* nature, and besides, this elevated moral duty or responsibility in the human relationship to nature is still expressive of a kind of species-egoism: nature is to be treated with care so that, primarily, *our* species may continue to survive and enjoy its unique and superior position also in the future. An important and relevant implication of the idea of the elevated species, furthermore – slowly maturing and surfacing in the European religious and idealistic tradition – is a sense of the *oneness* of the race, its shared predicament in the natural world and its common destiny. In spite of differences observed and encountered in actual existence – distinctions of language, ethnic type, colour, gender, prowess, virtue, intelligence, and the like – there is also an underlying or transcendent 'equality' which enjoins that human individuals – even wicked human individuals – are to be treated in a way different to other creatures.

This leads us to the fourth idea to be mentioned. This idea is the human *communtiy* which in terms of this perspective is assigned a supreme moral value. Community is of course not the same thing as 'communism' but this idea is nevertheless to be seen as the logical prerequisite of *all* communist doctrines we shall find in the Western tradition, including Marxism. It is evident that any society which is based on a system of sharing of material goods – which is the basic definition of communism – makes sense only on the assumption of a more fundamental kind of sharing, and 'sharing' not just as a projected desideratum but as a part of human reality, already existing. Communism clearly presupposes community and the reality and importance of 'communication', the sharing of minds, hearts, feelings, thoughts, desires, the presence of a level of existence and consciousness which expresses the unity of the race in the 'spiritual' as distinguished from the bare anthropological sense. Also, communication and company would in this perspective be presented as the highest kind of human satisfaction available; community is not just a means to other ends but the supreme end itself. It is through community – the cultivation and living of companionship – that human beings will come closest to the benevolent universe, achieve their highest transcendence. It is through community – the on-going cross-fertilization of minds – that humans have been able to produce and maintain both culture (inward excellence) and civilization (external potency) and thus achieve their elevation over other species. And community is the highest moral value: good conduct, thoughts and actions properly befitting members of the human race, are those which follow from and express conscious *identification* with fellow humans, which is to say moral preference given to an overarching and abstract 'humanity' as against the *mere* immediate and natural self, the self rooted in and shackled by the world of actual existence. Community is reason, heaven, true happiness, lordship over nature; isolation and mere 'individual' satisfaction are evil, the falsification of the human essence, continuing slavery to nature. Thus the idea of community, we might say, is the crowning and logical conclusion of the other three ideas mentioned: in it the benevolent universe, objective morality and the elevation of the species are brought together in a solemn and triumphant coda.

I need not emphasize once more that the foregoing description of a fundamental 'idealistic perspective' in European thought is a mental construct only, a heuristic device if you like, 'distilled' from available sources. *As such* it is not to be found in any single document or concrete 'school' of writing. The latter do contain these four ideas, to be sure, but in a great variety of contexts and in different formulations. Nothing can or should be expected to be neat and straightforward in the history of ideas, unless we are willing to 'distil'. In this instance I would maintain that no proper sense could be made of the deepest background – conception – of Marxism unless we formulated an idealistic perspective along these lines; the four basic ideas identified above *are* operative in the deep structure of Marxist thought – form part of its range of necessary presuppositions – and at the same time their presence *can* be detected in the unfolding Western tradition. I shall offer just a few, and rather obvious, illustrations from an immensely vast and complicated field.

In chronological order the first source to be mentioned is Old Testament Judaism, the sacred texts and fiery pronouncements of the ancient Hebrew prophets. Here we encounter, for the first time stated clearly and forcefully in our tradition – coming, incidentally, from the 'Orient' – the idea that moral conduct for humans is prescribed in the 'law' of the one God of Israel in whom the benevolence of the universe is concentrated and who maintains a personal, direct relationship to his 'chosen people'. Though in ancient Judaism the category, 'chosen people', tends to be described in ethnic terms, it has a strong moral element built into it, as those distinguished by 'righteous living', and it is in this way that the idea has become fertile and influential in the whole Western tradition. The people of God are to keep God's commandments: they are to worship the divine law-giver and to treat their fellows as they treat themselves; they are to be generous and neighbourly in their conduct, identifying with the community. The wicked will be punished by a just and omnipotent God whose ultimate triumph – the triumph of 'good' personified – is of course assured; the world of transcendence devours the world of actual existence; Jerusalem will outlive and destroy Babylon.

In the second place, and (advisedly in view of what is to follow) in somewhat greater detail, reference should be made here to classical idealist philosophy in Greece, and with particular attention to its greatest acknowledged representative, Plato. Many people have contended that Plato is the most outstanding Western philosopher who has ever lived, who as it were 'started the ball rolling' and more or less created the perspective of transcendence in European culture, and certainly in the realm of intellectual speculation. Some writers – and obviously this point is of special interest here – even argued that there has been a *direct* Platonic impact on the development of mainstream political ideologies in the modern age, notably those with 'totalitarian' tendencies, which would include Marxism. But here it is advisable to exercise some caution. The point I made earlier in connection with Marx's immediate predecessors applies generally, and with particular force in the case of alleged fundamental direct influences, like the Platonic: it will certainly not do to erect Plato as some kind of antediluvian, archetypal Marxist revolutionary, and nor will it be appropriate to narrow the 'essence' of Marxism into some kind of latter-day, modernized Platonism. There is more – much more – to Plato than an embryonic pointer towards modern radical thought, and there is definitely a great deal more to Marx than Platonic idealism (or Old Testament religion and moralism, for that matter), suitably transliterated.

Be that as it may, two notions found in Plato do deserve special emphasis here. The first is that which epitomizes Platonic philosophical 'idealism' in the proper sense: this is the view, to put it somewhat crudely, that the world of empirical reality – what we have been calling 'actual existence' here – is *secondary* in terms of logic as well as practical moral import to a transcendent world of 'ideas' or 'forms'. The significant point here is that for Plato human beings partake of this transcendent world by virtue of their *reason*, their rationality and intellect,

16

the power of their thought. At the pinnacle of human society stands the 'philosopher', the knower and lover of reason, who in his thought reaches beyond the empirical world around him, who achieves morality, goodness as well as satisfaction, through rationality. That Plato operates with a rigid hierarchy of human society – assuming and asserting substantive inequalities within the human race – is beside the point here. What is significant is his parallel hierarchy drawn between ways of life and valuations. The best life is the life of reason. And the second relevant notion to be found in Plato has to do with his description of the perfect city governed by reason. Philosophy and community for Plato are intrinsically related. On the one hand, philosophers, 'guardians', men and women of reason, are the best appointed – as it were 'natural' – rulers of the city by virtue exclusively of their transcendent vision, their ability to perceive and mete out impartial 'justice' in accordance with the immutable, objective, universal 'idea' of the good. It is therefore in the true interest of every inhabitant of the city, including inferior slaves, that philosophers should govern. And on the other hand the rulers themselves derive their highest satisfaction through thus ruling impartially, for no material reward, in complete identification with and selflessly 'serving' the community. Plato's so-called 'communism' here enters the picture. As Plato sets it out in the pages of *The Republic*, the guardians in the ideal city must not possess any private property or live in individual households, in restricted familial relationships. They are to be one with the community and the community achieves its highest excellence through their thoughts and their lives. Thus, if you like, in Platonic philosophy the two 'universals' or basic ideas of the perspective outlined above are already explicitly united: the universal of reason and the universal of human fellowship. We are, of course, still *very far* removed from modern 'communism', or from Marx's (and, pointedly, Lenin's) perspective of the membership of the 'Communist Party', with its 'advanced consciousness' and role of revolutionary leadership, appointed by history. It is sheer solecism to see a direct connection here. However, what *is* valid and relevant and has to be asserted is necessary connection of an indirect and negative nature: such doctrines as Marxist communism would be scarcely if at all conceivable in a cultural tradition which did not count Plato's writings among its most respected and influential inheritances.

Christianity, obviously, also figures as an important source in the unfolding perspective of transcendence. Having emerged out of the tribal religion of the Hebrews, adding a New Testament to the Old, Christianity proceeded to extend and in an important sense 'revolutionize' the ideas of a divinely ordained morality and the chosen people. The operative principle of the latter now becomes wholly 'spiritual' and moral (i.e detribalized): God's people are the pure in heart, Jews as well as Gentiles, who observe the 'law' and who in addition are enjoined to love also their enemies and follow the Saviour in the path of willing self-renunciation and sacrifice. Unlike Judaism, Christianity has a kind of sublime cultural 'imperialism' built deeply into it: God's people are their 'brothers' keepers', they have a responsibility for the salvation of the souls of others, not only their own, their mission is to the whole of the human race, they have to proselytize, spread the faith, endeavour to establish as much of the 'kingdom' on earth as is humanly possible. Furthermore, Christianity contains a very resolute and emphatic rejection of the world of 'actual existence', with pointed reference to the world of 'Mammon'. The Sermon on the Mount declares the spirit of poverty to be positive happiness, the gateway to heaven, and here too we find the profoundly revolutionary message concerning the meek who will inherit the earth. And note that although Christianity has crystallized over the centuries as a 'religion' with an 'otherworldly' orientation, and institutionalized as a 'church' with an increasingly marginalized and subordinate role in politics, it has always contained a strong *political* and *radical* undercurrent. This was so quite pronouncedly at the very beginning when the 'poor' and the 'meek', oppressed and persecuted in the Roman Empire, set out to establish God's kingdom in a spirit of brotherly sharing and conditions of material communism; and in certain periods afterwards (e.g. preceding as well as following the Reformation). But even if we were to discount this political and directly revolutionary aspect, Christianity would still loom very significantly in the story of the genesis of Marxism, on account of the *dignity* that its teaching (though not invariably its practice) has bestowed on 'lowly' forms of human life, accompanied by the *hope* that – some day, somewhere and in some form – the wheel will turn full circle and present suffering and degradation will be rewarded by eternal bliss. Again, there are a lot of gaps to be filled, quite a few further stories to be told, before we reach and can begin fully to comprehend such a complicated modern concept as Marx's 'proletariat' – but the 'meek' and 'poor' of Christianity, with their dignity and transcendent hope, are assuredly there at the foundations.

The principle of human *equality*, in my view, underlies just about everything that is distinctive and weighty and worthy in the mainstream of our tradition. This principle first emerged in the ancient world, born as the offspring of the marriage between Christianity and classical philosophy. With Stoicism, the 'religion' of intellectuals in the pagan Roman Empire, we already see a decisive shift effected from the Platonic idealistic outlook of human hierarchy to one of basic human equality, on the level of 'reason', declared to be the common possession of the species. It is noteworthy, however, that Stoic perspective still includes a hierarchy of ways of life, in the manner of Plato, pronouncing 'wisdom' to be the highest human quality. From the very beginning it was a major principle of Christian doctrine that all human beings were basically equal 'in the sight of God', all possessing (and being unique in this respect among natural species) an 'immortal soul'. The philosophical 'education' of Christianity came to the fore already in the Pauline perspective and achieved its highest early peak in the writings of Saint Augustine, the Christian political thinker *par excellence*, who has also been credited with being the first 'philosopher of history' in the European tradition; a point which is of course not entirely without significance in the present context. In Augustine's tremendous work, *The City of God*, the Christian view of human equality and human dignity is outlined with force and eloquence, Augustine resolutely rejecting the principle of slavery. We find here also an emphatic condemnation of unjust and oppressive government – again, in terms of grand principle and the tone echoing that of the ancient Hebrew prophets – with Augustine likening tyrannical rulers to the leaders of criminal gangs. The divine city of the righteous and the pure in heart is sharply contrasted to *actual existence*, the mundane city of vice, godlessness, egoism, materialism, oppression and violence. And although it is stated in heavy and poetic theological language, there is definitely a view of human progress coming into evidence, a vision of the human species moving in one determinate direction over the centuries, out of darkness and towards the light, the original Fall of the human race having been redeemed once and for all through Christ's early presence, death and resurrection, and the way to eventual salvation now lying open.

As with Platonic idealism and communism, and the Gospel espousal of poverty, again we have to exercise a certain amount of caution lest we read too much into these early views. The Stoic and early Christian principle of equality is *not* quite the same as the modern principle. The Augustinian view of history is *not* the view of Condorcet, Millar, Hegel or Marx. Equality with the former is still 'spiritual', operative behind the scenes as it were, and with little direct practical relevance to government and social relations; historical progression in Augustine does not mean progressive liberation from autocratic rulers and stifling customs or the increase of material prosperity. For these further advances we have to await the onset of the modern period. But it is still the case that modern ideas are and must be seen to be based on these earlier harbingers; without the presence of these in the tradition no 'advances' could have been made – or they would have been radically different. Equality of moral responsibility – which is the quintessential core of the Christian view – is without any doubt presupposed by modern doctrines of legal, political and social equality; otherwise these would make no sense whatsoever. Only *equally transcendent* individual units (i.e. all having an 'immortal soul') can logically and reasonably claim a formally (and *a fortiori* substantively) equal access to societal decision-making and other provisions. And no doctrine of historical progress would carry any conviction unless an *idea* of transcendence were injected into it from the very start: in this case it is certainly the transference of the idea of individual redemption and resurrection on to the plane of human society. How the transference comes about in modern European thought we shall see later.

So much, then, for some of the actual historical sources of the perspective which I have called here the tradition of 'transcendence' in European thought and which I am suggesting is – *in part* – responsible for the earliest 'conception' of Marxism. The point to make is that the four key ideas which I ventured to distil from Judaeo-Christian and Greco-Roman sources did not become 'prunes', withering away with the demise of the classical and medieval periods. On the very contrary, the notions of the benevolent universe, objective morality, the human species with a unique nature and destiny, and the positive value of the community, have not only lived on and prospered but have become the *absolute presuppositions* (to adapt this well-known term of R. G. Collingwood's) of modern radical thought, including Marxist thought. Marxism – and I shall be bold enough to assert this categorically – would be *meaningless* in the absence of these presuppositions at its very base. However, I will hasten to add the further and vitally important point: Marxism would also be meaningless – or at least very considerably weakened as an intellectual construct – if it contained the assumptions of transcendence *only*. Marxism is a modernized version of the European religious perspective *plus*, and so our task is to outline in a rudimentary way the basic features of this 'plus', also to be uncovered in the deepest layers of our cultural inheritance. However, it is important for us to note not only *that* there is another perspective – the perspective of science, of realism – but also *why* it is there, i.e. its ultimate rationale. And the handiest way to indicate this, it seems to me, is to call attention to the problematic nature of the key ideas located in the perspective of transcendence. The truth, of course, is that the ideas of the benevolent universe, objective morality, the elevated species and the community are certainly very moving, very inspiring, very sublime, very influential ideas – but they hang in mid-air. The perspective of transcendence invites *criticism* and is definitely in need of complementation.

It will, I think, be in order to raise a few critical questions right here, for the ideas concerned are built into the foundations of Marxism, although to some extent hidden from view there by the elaborate architectual ornaments of the Marxist edifice. Thus at least we shall gain an early glimpse here – before the story of the genesis of Marxism is entered into in earnest – of some of the bigger problems facing Marxist thought at its base. Taking these ideas in reverse order, we can ask for instance whether or not the move from 'community' to 'communism' is warranted. Community by itself signifies very little: *everybody* pays lip-service to community and is in favour of 'identifying' with the species, in some vague, remote, abstract and impractical sense, everybody likes to 'communicate' and enjoy the company of others. But nothing at all follows from this. The 'sharing' of important things in life, like material goods and marriage-partners, is quite a different matter and what seems to be in the way of realizing this sublime ideal is 'actual existence' itself which, whatever it is, is *not* 'communist' in the required sense. The present *facts* of egoism, cupidity, possessiveness, can be treated with contempt but they cannot simply just be 'spirited' away. How do we and why *should* we ever move from A to B? The point is that the perspective of transcendence, on its own, cannot supply an adequate answer: by its very purity and majestic distance from the here and now, it also implicitly acknowledges its impotence *vis à vis* actual existence.

Then, concerning the alleged uniqueness and elevation of our species, the question can and should be asked: what, after all, is so special and so marvellous about humans? Is it their 'reason'? Nobody has yet been able to demonstrate that human intelligence and human understanding are anything but quantitatively different – 'larger' if you like – from the ways in which other species in nature have come to terms with their predicament. If anything, human beings have shown themselves to be less 'adaptable' to their environment than species of animals. Or is it the capacity of human beings to achieve 'goodness', to transcend their individual selves and identify with the community? That is, surely, absurd. Human beings, if anything, can be most easily distinguished from other species by their universally displayed *intra-specific* conflict and aggression. So in the last resort it may be that the most complimentary thing to be said about the human race is that it is an animal species, no better and no worse than others found in nature. But of course this observation, if taken seriously, has extremely important implications for the radical transcendent vision, including the

Marxist vision: animal species may not have private property, class divisions, oppression and exploitation but they are definitely not 'communistic' either. So why should we expect just this one animal species to be different?

We do not seem to fare much better with the other two key ideas either. Our great religions and trend-setting philosophies (like Plato's) have maintained that good and evil are something *objective*, given, universal and eternal, parts of the universe like the earth and the stars. But is this view valid or indeed intelligible, beyond the level of vague and inconsequential generalities? Again, there are grave problems encountered in surveying the world of 'actual existence' which has of course always shown an immense variety and instability of moral codes and practices. These can be reduced to a common denominator only at the expense of giving up any concreteness and practicality. In the last resort, objective morality is either tautologous (i.e. good is good, evil is evil) or false. Now would this observation not suggest that there may be an irreducible element of *subjective* and *contingent* valuation in moral experience, in our understanding of good and evil? That these are not really parts of the universe but simply – and always ambiguously – follow from historically varied and contingent circumstances? And of course if this is the case, then once again a serious doubt is raised in regard to visionary ideals like communism. If morality is subjective in this basic sense, then there is no *compelling* reason why a life of sharing, co-operation, altruism should ever be preferred to the life experienced in actual existence or why this remote ideal should be fought for. Lastly, it is quite obvious that any argument concerning the 'benevolence' of the universe would be incapable of demonstration. This is and remains a matter of faith rather than intellectual conviction. Even if we were to grant it – for the sake of argument – that the universe has *so far* conducted itself quite 'benevolently' towards the human race – otherwise we wouldn't be here to tell the story! – it would still not follow that things will be the same in future. And once again: if the benevolence of the universe is not assured, if we have to accept that the future is literally open, and ultimate reality essentially opaque, then what is the *point* of striving and struggle, of sacrificing the small change of actual existence for the shiny prize of an ideal society that may *never* come about? If Western religion has had to struggle with this problem – the problem of making 'heaven' intelligible – then of course we must note that Western political theory, with its 'earthly heaven' as an integral aspect of the modern radical vision, has had an even more desperate struggle on its hands.

I posed these critical questions here rather starkly, following on an equally stark, not to say 'robust', introduction of key ideas in what I have been calling the perspective of transcendence. These ideas are to be found at the very bottom of the *visionary* aspect of Marxist doctrine. The point of view of transcendence informs both the Marxist critique of the capitalist system of production and the bourgeois social order (i.e 'actual existence') and the constructive, future-oriented aspects of Marxism, i.e. the anticipated proletarian revolution, the building of socialist society, the arrival of communism, etc. In the preceding paragraphs I attempted to show that these ideas of transcendence in Marxism, the 'bricks' or 'foundation-stones', are in themselves shaky, wanting. What is missing still is as it were the 'cement' holding the bricks together. This cement, I would now like to argue, comes to Marxism through successive adaptations and development of the other fundamental perspective of European thought defined here as the perspective of *understanding* and science. I shall now turn to this alternative tradition. But let me make two preliminary remarks. Firstly, it is not to be imagined that these two great planks of our cultural inheritance stand simply in a relationship of 'end and means' to each other, with religion setting the aim and science providing the know-how. In truth the two overlap, cross-fertilize and interpenetrate at every step in the unfolding of European thought and society. Secondly, and related to this, it is not to be presumed that these two perspectives *either* smoothly dovetail, complementing each other *or* directly clash, one contradicting the other. The truth is – difficult maybe, but important to grasp if we want to make proper sense of the genesis of Marxism – that they co-exist in a state of permanent *tension*, pushing together and at the same time pulling apart. Later on we shall see this tension present in the 'gestation' and 'formation' as well as the 'fruition' of Marxism, a doctrine in which the two points of view are *just about* held together.

The gist of this other perspective in Western political and social theory is the view that the ever-increasing knowledge of the workings of nature (external as well as human nature) will make the radical transformation of the conditions of human life and the organization of society possible, warranted and indeed imminent. Here the departure is not any outlying idea of an objective 'good', a benevolent universe, an elevated species, the value of community, or anything like that, but the world of *actual existence* itself, the tangible here and now of human wishes, the desire for enjoyment, immediate happiness, all-sided gratification. What this perspective tells us, broadly speaking, is that the things we 'naturally' desire – enough food and drink, shelter from the weather, outlets for sexual gratification, interesting activities, exciting company and partnership: in short, 'bread and circuses' in plenty and in perpetuity – are *attainable*, we can have them. What we encounter here, if you like, is an illumination of the distinctive Western idea of freedom 'from below': freedom is essentially and primarily freedom from want, from fear, from being shackled by our present (but van- ishing) ignorance of nature. I am purposely stressing here the 'materialistic' side of human aspirations because these – 'base' and 'vulgar' as they might be (in fact, in some moods, Marx himself thought so) – are at the same time *basic* both to the popular appeal and to the intellectual coherence of Marxism. In Marxism communal identification and moral transcendence on the one hand, and material plenty and 'natural' individual satisfaction on the other, go together. The sublime and the basic – the ideal 'pull' and the natural 'push' – are in this doctrine at least in principle *reconciled*. The Marxist enterprise, succinctly but I hope not too crudely interpreted, consists pre- cisely in the bringing down of heaven effected by the sim- ultaneous raising of the earth, the realization of the aspirations of the *natural* human being in the framework of an *ideal* organ- ization of society.

Let us then attempt to break down this perspective schem- atically, as we did with the perspective of transcendence. I shall identify or 'distil' three key ideas involved here, which (only partly for the sake of dramatic presentation) I am going to call three *cool looks*. In the first place we will find here a cool look at external nature itself. Nature in this perspective comes to the fore essentially as a proper object of study and understanding: the natural world is knowable and hence manageable, it can be tamed, pacified and – given sufficient learning – conquered. Note that here, in contradistinction to the other perspective, the stress is not on any supposed overall 'rationality' of the universe, and even less on its 'benevolence', but on the possibility of learning about nature *in detail*, by working our way up from observed facts to general conclusions. With patience and an 'open mind' we shall succeed in this endeavour to the very limits of the natural equipment of the human being, i.e. the ability to observe and make experiments, to store and connect bits of information, to think logically, to make practical use of knowledge thus accumulated. Nature or reality here comes to view as being essentially – if not exclusively – 'spatio-temporal', i.e. 'material' in the relevant sense, a 'system' where everything somehow hangs together and where, therefore, the understanding of one part relates to the understanding of other parts. Nature behaves in a 'law-like' manner, can be likened to an artifact or machine which can be taken to parts and reassembled again. Nature has no mystical dimension, no transcendence in it; once known, it can be manipulated; faith becomes gradually superfluous in the process of advancing knowledge; the human intellect *unaided* suffices for the tasks set by natural human aspirations. Instead of being benevolent, nature is neutral, indifferent: there is no cosmic guarantee for the ultimate success of human endeavour but on the other hand there is a modest, yet firm, confidence that the growth of human knowledge will lead at the very minimum to the diminution of the present *fear* of nature.

In the second place, we encounter here a cool look at human society. As nature is neutral and indifferent, so is society. It is first and foremost a proper object of study, perfectly amenable to understanding and consequent management. Society is not to be approached in lofty moral terms, it is not to be seen as an arena for the waging of a cosmic conflict between good and evil. The nature and problems of society can and must be comprehended within the confines of society, on its own terms.

There is nothing mysterious about the institutions of government, law, war and peace, economic activity, education or the family. We do not need to have recourse to such moral and value-laden notions as justice, authority and obligation in order to understand the springs of human action in society and the relationship between individuals and groups. The production, distribution and exchange of societal goods – material, political, cultural and any other kind – occur also, as with external nature, in a 'law-like' manner, consequently they can be studied scientifically, by recourse to logic and empirical observation. Human beings in society are primarily motivated by what they see (rightly or wrongly) as their 'interests' in the world of actual existence; as their interests are not normally harmonious there is 'conflict' in society; the outcome of actions on the collective level is a variety of settlements which are to be understood in terms of 'power', i.e. some individuals or groups impose their interest and rule on others and the latter, for the time being, have no choice but to endure the situation.

In the third place, we find here a cool look at human values, morality and the nature of the 'good society', social and political aims to work for. The important point here is the derivation of values from human interests, wants, desires, needs, as experienced in the world of actual existence. Morality is not 'given' from above but built up from below. What human beings desire *now*, to better their life conditions and achieve 'happiness', is broadly speaking *all right*, fully justified and to be promoted. Morality is what is conducive to the attainment of satisfaction; there is nothing else important or intelligible in the ideas of good and evil, right and wrong. We find here also a principle of equality – or perhaps rather what is a rough-and-ready assumption of equality – which is quite different from equality as understood in the religious perspective and its derivatives. There equality is 'in the sight of God', i.e. transcendent, whereas here it is equality as it were 'in the sight of nature', referring to the broad comparability of human appetites, natural instincts, potentialities and limitations. Other things being equal, the proper aim therefore is the widest possible spreading of satisfactions, and their intensification. Happiness consists for the most part in *consumption* (of whatever kind of goods) by individuals, and society exists chiefly so that all goods wanted may be efficiently produced and distributed. The achievement of material prosperity, though it may not be the ultimate end, is still the most important concrete objective; in a situation of material plenty individual and group 'interests' can be satisfied, so that there is a diminution or possibly elimination, of 'conflict', and hence the role of 'power' also changes. All that is needed is the rational, functional organization of society, based on our knowledge of society.

One of the most acute among modern observers and theorists of society, Emile Durkheim, once defined 'socialism' precisely in the above terms, contrasting it sharply to an older tradition of 'communism'. The former, socialism, is essentially about prosperity and rational organization, whereas the latter is about sharing and identification in conditions of 'saintly poverty'. In the scheme of these lectures (or more precisely this first lecture) the first would roughly correspond to what I have called the perspective of understanding and the second to the perspective of transcendence. There is at least one good reason for presenting these two in the way I have done here, namely that in Marxism *both* are present, closely intertwined and well-nigh inseparable. One particular area in which this close convergence and interpenetration can be observed – and this is directly relevant to the third 'cool look' we have been considering – is production. In Marxist doctrine human production or labour comes to view almost as 'divine' activity, a mark of the nobility of man, *the* crucial characteristic distinguishing humans from animals, an act of 'creation'. And production is at the same time presented as mundane 'natural' activity, a necessary and ordinary aspect of human life, engaged in solely so that individuals may actually obtain and consume what they need and desire, and thus acquire happiness.

So much then for the underlying ideas of this perspective. Perhaps I should make here the observation that – as it has no doubt appeared clearly in the foregoing – with science and understanding there is no way in which to identify a 'tradition' in exactly the same sense in which one can describe the idealistic-religious inheritance. I have, in my brief characterization of the three 'cool looks' above, purposely (and to some extent unavoidably) used the *language* of modernity. It is certainly the case that, at least at first glance, the scientific-realistic attitude – and the perspective of social science in particular – would appear to be a characteristic product of the modern age, in fact *defining* the modern age in contradistinction to earlier phases of Western civilization. But this is not entirely so. A much better way of explaining the situation would be to say that in our intellectual heritage the perspective of transcendence *peaks* earlier than the perspective of understanding, the former then dominating the latter – while it is, more or less, the other way round in the modern age. It is, therefore, important for us to note in this discussion of the original 'conception' of Marxist doctrine that – fragmentary or not, subdued or not – there *are* visible chunks of this second perspective also to be found in the earliest phases of European culture, almost coeval with the appearance of the religious perspective. I shall very briefly refer to a few of these chunks. Two pertinent illustrations, to begin with, can be taken from classical Greco-Roman philosophy. Firstly, in the materialist philosophy of Epicurus we do find a view of nature and human values which can hardly be surpassed in their 'coolness'. Note that Epicurus was one of Marx's greatest heroes, called in the latter's doctoral dissertation the outstanding figure of the ancient Greek 'enlightenment'. Marx, as a matter of fact, was then more interested in the Epicurean theory of 'swerving atoms' in the universe than in Epicurean social and moral philosophy. But this philosophy, as can be gleaned from the memorable poem of Lucretius, *De Rerum Natura*, does propound a view of nature, human nature and human values which must be seen as an alternative foundation to Platonism, sowing the seeds of another tradition or perspective. Human fulfilment and happiness, in the Epicurean scheme, come as a result of the understanding of nature. In the Epicurean universe there is no spiritual reality, no transcendent deity, no personal immortality; there is only the world of *actual existence*, the here and now which can be, once the fear of nature is banished from the human mind, actually enjoyed. The message, at first subdued but of course becoming dominant in the modern age, is simple and robust: come to terms with this world, there is nothing else to follow.

We can take as our second illustration here some elements

found in Aristotle's philosophy. The choice might seem a bit strange at first, for Aristotle was a disciple of Plato and thus, in significant ways, partaker also of the idealistic tradition of transcendence. Besides, unlike Epicurus, Aristotle was certainly not one of Marx's heroes, though Marx knew his philosophy intimately. For the most part, Aristotle is treated critically in Marx's writings. Nevertheless, latter-day students of Marx have unquestionably been correct in calling attention to the heavy deep-structural influence of Aristotelian thought on Marxism, some of which of course would have got to Marx via Hegel. In the present context, however, I think it is enough for us just to note this in passing. Emphasis should fall here instead on two aspects of Aristotelian philosophy which appear to be particularly important for a developing perspective of understanding in European thought. The first concerns Aristotle's notion of the 'good life' which, in contradistinction to Platonic transcendence, is defined in terms of balanced satisfactions, and with a mundane, this-worldly orientation. Aristotle's perspective on values and on society is certainly cool and commonsensical; he is much more interested in what is attainable, projecting out of actual existence, than with the ideal and abstractly desirable. The second, and indeed even more noteworthy, aspect is Aristotle's scientific and conflictual view of society and government. Though by no means indifferent to moral and social 'values', Aristotle has the deadpan, cool approach of the student, searching out variables, considering causes and effects. Not only does he classify political units, i.e. states, in terms of the nature of *power* wielded in them but – and this point is of great significance here, for us – he defines conflicting groups within these units in terms of their *social* position, i.e. their differential possession of material wealth. For Aristotle the basic conflict in society is the conflict between the rich and the poor. Now needless to say it would be just as dangerous and misleading to read some sort of antediluvian Marxist doctrine of the 'class struggle' into Aristotle as it would be to set up Plato as a fully-fledged spiritual 'communist'. However, as with Plato's thought, the relevance of the Aristotelian doctrine of social conflict for a developing perspective of *cool* understanding of society is pretty obvious; not Marx, and not even Marx's modern predecessors, were the first to focus on conflict as the key concept in the scientific study of society. Just as with salvation and transcendence, so this perspective and its characteristic preoccupations – with interest, conflict and power – also derive from the past, from the European mainstream.

The point has been made earlier that the tradition of science, realism, understanding lay dormant – subdued, overshadowed – for a long period of European history, coming into its own and indeed becoming the dominating partner with the onset of the modern age only. Modernity, however, was heralded in before the 'scientific revolution' of the sixteenth century by the *Renaissance*, truly and consciously a 'rebirth' of the classical spirit. In the field of political theory this spirit was most dramatically expressed in the writings of Niccolò Machiavelli who could conveniently serve as our third and last illustration of this emerging perspective before the coming of the modern age. Machiavelli's secularism, republicanism and his notorious view of political morality provide the bridge between the classical origins and modern flowering of the perspective of understanding. Often called the first 'modern' political thinker, Machiavelli unites the three 'cool looks' we have identified earlier as being central to this outlook. His view of nature is serene and sombre, and his 'universe' is anything but 'benevolent'. He has a chilling, hardheaded, no-nonsense approach to society and government, relentlessly emphasizing the central role of power. And his values and vision are thoroughly secular, based on the perceived desires and satisfactions of people in their actual existence. The Machiavellian roots of Marx's theory of social conflict and change are of course easily recognizable, though surprisingly perhaps it took a fairly long time for Marx-scholarship to attain to this level of 'genetical' interpretation. But it is certainly not an inexplicable historical accident that the thinker widely (and rightly) regarded as *the* outstanding Marxist philosopher of the twentieth century, Antonio Gramsci, should have erected Machiavellism into a central pillar of his theories.

Now, before we proceed further to complete the story of the conception of Marxism, perhaps a few critical questions could be raised also in respect of the central ideas in the perspective of understanding. I attempted earlier to suggest reasons why a perspective of science and realism *has* to be invoked in a discussion of the genesis of Marxism. The simple reason is that the root ideas of the Marxist vision – the ideas of transcendence – are wanting and incomplete and unconvincing in themselves; they 'hang in mid-air'. But it is by no means difficult to see that the 'cool looks' involved in this second perspective are also wanting in themselves and require not just 'reasoning' but – I am sorry to say – a certain amount of *faith* before they can be accepted as valid, either as the proper tools of human understanding or reliable guidelines to political action. And again this brief critical exercise will be no idle luxury in our overall context: Marxism *is* a development of this perspective as well as of the previous one.

In the first place, the 'cool look' at nature would – it certainly should – raise some eyebrows these days. Is it at all conceivable that our 'increasing' knowledge of nature, and apparent 'mastery' of it (through technology, etc.), are in principle *finite* processes which one day will come to a triumphant conclusion, so that thereafter we can sit back in comfort and continuously enjoy our omniscience and omnipotence? Even posing the question this way, let alone giving an affirmative answer, would sound absurd. Yet we must note that something *like* an affirmative answer is implied in many of the assertions made on behalf of Marxism, and sometimes (in Engels' *Anti-Dühring* for instance) this optimistic faith in the growth of knowledge and its consequences is explicitly avowed. In the perspective of Marx's and Engels' generation of radical thinkers and 'scientific' critics of society it was, more or less, taken for granted that human knowledge *was* advancing with giant leaps, that it was cumulative with a finite end in view, and that consequently the human species was *really*, literally, 'ascending' out of a state of ignorance and barbarism towards the cool and comforting light of scientific knowledge. The understanding and mastery of human life and society were thought to be firmly based on the knowledge of nature. Today, to say the least, this view would appear rather naive and starry-eyed. Nowadays increasing sophistication in our understanding of nature will tend rather to be accompanied by tempered confidence and a growing sense of awe and even mystery. There is no foreseeable 'end' to the growth of knowledge; new advances and new discoveries lead to fresh problems, new planes of ignorance. What difference does this – as it were more 'mature' – conception of the nature of human knowledge make to the appeal, validity, intellectual force of Marxism? I think on the whole Marxism is being rendered more vulnerable and more exposed in this new atmosphere, with its erstwhile air of optimism and certainty – benefiting from the air of certainty and optimism bestowed on natural science in the nineteenth century – having been slowly eroded. At the same time it must be noted that Marxism is not meant to be the science *of nature* directly as such, and thus it is not inexorably tied to any one particular natural science paradigm (e.g. Newtonian physics, Darwinian biology); in this regard it can certainly afford to be flexible. We can make one pertinent remark here at any rate: to a great extent, if not wholly, the subsequent development of Marxist doctrine, especially from the mid-twentieth century onwards, has consisted in a series of attempts by eminent thinkers to *explain away* the simplistic scientific optimism built into their chosen outlook right from its inception, and the task has not been found too easy.

There are also considerable doubts concerning the idea that some day (and not very far removed in time) we shall possess a perfect knowledge of society and shall consequently be able to organize society in accordance with rational and scientific understanding. Is scientific government conceivable? Is human society like a book to be read and learnt by heart? What this view implies at bottom of course is that human action and conduct in society, and social structures, processes and relationships, are *essentially* like phenomena found in nature (and assuming of course that nature, too, can be thus read and learnt). And this in turn amounts to an implicit denial of any kind of 'transcendence' and of some – fairly important – senses of human *freedom*. A science of society means that, in the last analysis, human beings are governed by natural necessity. Now, to say the least, it has been less than easy to demonstrate the validity of this assertion in the light of the experience of 'actual existence', and of course social science must *start out* from actual existence. But here we encounter such awkward, disturbing facts as unpredictability, inconsistency, spontaneity, irrationality and self-contradiction universally displayed in human conduct. How is it possible to account for these? How is it conceivable that they can be overcome and eliminated? It might appear simple at first to say that they are the result of 'insufficient knowledge', in principle remediable; it is much more difficult actually to hit upon the remedy.

After some three thousand years of scientific speculation, and three hundred years of modern Enlightenment, the big 'breakthrough' to the scientific management of society has still not arrived. Now what does *this* observation tell us about Marxism? It is undeniable that Marxism did come to fruition in this confident modern social science atmosphere, offering *the* infallible remedy, *the* principle of explanation which would render human conduct and the processes and structures of society 'transparent'. Again, we should avoid the temptation to go overboard on this: fortunately (for us as students of Marx) there is a great deal more in Marxist doctrine than this element of assertive and confident scientism. The whole of Marxism, particularly visible but not confined to Marx's early writings, is shot through with ideas belonging to a perspective of trans-cendence. However, the critical observation made in the pre-vious paragraph applies here, too, and indeed with greater assurance and emphasis: on the whole Marxism is meant to be the science *of society*, though not the science of nature, and in the field of society it has operated its own distinctive paradigm. Experience has not been overwhelmingly kind to this paradigm and, mainly for this reason, Marxism has since its foundation had to undergo a series of 'dilutions', all having the effect of diminishing its social scientific character, its confidence in making accurate predictions and offering invincible panaceas. The more sophisticated, the more 'philosophical', the more 'mature', the more 'academic' Marxism has become – and who would deny that Marxism has become all that? – the more its own genetical background on this side, that is to say the whole European tradition of science, understanding, realism and Enlightenment, has been thrown into disarray, becoming almost an embarrassment.

Finally the 'cool look' at human values and morality would certainly leave a lot of people rather cold – myself not excluded. It is highly doubtful if any kind of 'hedonism', however moderate and enlightened, or any kind of 'humanism', however benign and altruistic, could ever supply an adequate foundation of values or a convincing account of moral experience as we have known it in our civilization. Of course we are all, to a very considerable extent, practical 'Epicureans' in the sense of desiring and working for the 'good life' in terms of immediate, palpable satisfactions, both physical and mental. But values and morality don't simply follow from this: the observance of moral rules is scarcely, if ever, *automatic*, untroubled, spontaneous. The mere fact that it is usually not very easy to forego palpable and immediate satisfactions for the sake of general moral principles (e.g. truthfulness, respect for life, helping one's neighbour, etc.) seems to me to suggest that morality inevitably involves some kind of *transcendence*, whichever way we might be inclined to define it.

At this point we begin – it may be with some reluctance – our *return journey* towards the religious and idealistic foundations of our culture. The inadequacy of hedonistic and humanistic morality is in actual fact best demonstrated by the example of Marxism. It is precisely the hard, worldly, utterly secular and assertively materialistic dominant perspective within Marxism that has shown itself most dramatically in need of a principle of transcendence, an outlying aim and vision which are *not* – against appearances – derived from or translatable into the small change of desires and satisfactions experienced in the world of actual existence. This principle of transcendence in Marxism has been very successful indeed in evoking a spirit of sacrifice and self-abnegation on the part of generations of adherents whose attitude has often, and rightly, been likened to that of the early Christian martyrs. No 'cool look' on anything, nature, society, or human values, could on its own have produced anything like this.

*   *   *

The point I was trying to make in the foregoing section was that the earliest conception of Marxism might most advantageously be approached in *dualistic* terms, as outlined above. That is to say, Marx's thought may be considered a 'synthesis' of the two underlying perspectives of transcendence and understanding, *before* it is judged to be the synthesis of the three modern doctrines of political economy, socialist theory and humanist philosophy. The construction or 'distillation' of the two perspectives was necessary in order to show the historical character of the modern outlook itself, i.e. that it had not come 'out of the blue' but emerged from earlier foundations in Western culture. Now the one remaining task of this lecture, as already hinted, is to indicate briefly the path through which the two fundamental perspectives come together in the modern age to produce the general outlook which, in time, will spawn Marxism and of which, in a certain sense, Marxism can be seen as the highest culmination. The important point to grasp of course is that the modern outlook – and *a fortiori* the standpoint of 'enlightened' and critical radicalism (the immediate parent of Marxism) – is already 'synthetic'. It combines the perspectives of heaven and earth, the transcendent and the mundane, the visionary and the scientific, idealism and realism in a seemingly seamless web – which is the reason why I thought it advisable to present the two underlying perspectives in analytical separation, so as to highlight not only their potential complementarity but also the tension between them. Let us then, in a rudimentary fashion, survey some of the most important landmarks in this process of modern convergence.

The Reformation, in the first place, already expresses the 'coming down to earth' of Christianity; spiritual intensification goes together with the loosening of hierarchical structure. With Luther we get the doctrine of the 'priesthood of the individual believer', emphasis on 'faith' and 'works', on active Christianity, going with the critique of the commercialization and corruption of the Roman Church. With Calvin we get the emphasis on the self-governing Christian community, the 'theocracy' of the righteous. The so-called 'Protestant spirit', whether or not it is directly connected to 'capitalism', is certainly the spirit of *heavenly worldliness*, of justifying the ways of God by achieving success – including material success – in the here and now. Even the Protestant doctrine of 'predestination', seemingly at variance with the oncoming modern doctrines of equality, democracy and popular sovereignty, is relevant in a consideration of the origins of modern revolutionary creeds. The conception of a righteous 'elect' is not very far removed, either in time or in spirit, from later revolutionary 'vanguards' and 'elites' in 'republics of virtue', exercising 'educational dictatorship' over the backward (i.e. reprobate) masses. Several historians of ideas – with some exaggeration and bias, perhaps – have in fact traced a direct line of descent from Puritan and Calvinist religious self-righteousness through Jacobinism to the Blanquist, Marxist and Leninist notions of the dictatorship of the proletariat. But this belongs to a later part of our story.

The main point of interest to note here is that already in the sixteenth and (notably) seventeenth centuries there is a *radical* Protestantism on hand – the leftwing of the Reformation – in which the spiritual and religious ideas of the earlier reformers are pushed to their ultimate logical conclusion and are transformed, in their surging content, if not in their form, into secular and political ideas. Influenced by secular events as well as the advancement of science and philosophy (of which see below), these radical thinkers and movements now make a conscious attempt to 'turn the world upside down', in the biblical phrase (which also serves as the title of Christopher Hill's excellent account of radical Christianity in this period). These devout Christian believers take the 'political' message of the Scriptures seriously and literally set out to realize heaven on earth, in a renewed spate of fanatical millenarianism coupled with social radicalism, extolling the values of community and poverty, and angrily denouncing wealth and the wealthy. Community does lead to communism in the doctrine and practice, for example, of Münzer's Anabaptists and Winstanley's True Levellers. Or as Peter Riedemann, of the Moravian Brethren, says in his 'Account of our Religion' (1545):

> ... the communion of saints itself must show itself not
> only in spiritual but also in temporal things; that as Paul

saith, one might not have abundance and another suffer want, but that there may be equality.

The 'community of saints' has no longer a need for an institutionalized church, hierarchy and rituals to mediate between the world and divinity. Moreover it has less and less need for a static, *revealed* doctrine of religion to communicate the truths and values of divinity, the nature of transcendence. In what is undoubtedly one of the greatest of 'transformations' of European thought – the actual birth of modernity – radical religion itself *visibly* and *directly* changes into secular philosophy and radical politics. The tremendous significance of this change for a proper understanding of modern radicalism – and Marxism in particular – is I think still not sufficiently appreciated in the usual run of textbooks and historical accounts which instead stress absolute 'breaks' and 'watersheds' occurring at this time; although there are useful pointers, like Hill's book, mentioned above. The radical Protestant perspective more and more pushes human *reason* to the forefront, the unaided, natural capacity of human beings, reason which itself contains the divine spark of transcendence. Reason is direct communication with God, it is itself transcendence. Scripture is thus overshadowed and eventually replaced by secular thought, just as politics, actually 'living' the Gospel, replaces outward religious observances. The momentous convergence of the two great European traditions, of transcendence and understanding, is already in full sight: human rationality as found in actual existence reaches up to the heavens in a mighty effort to unite the two worlds.

It is from this point on that Christianity in the narrower sense, i.e. the churches and the doctrine, begins its slow process of retreat from the centre of the stage in the development of European thought and society. Of course it remains (and is) 'relevant' in many important ways but leadership nevertheless now passes on to secular, and intently secularizing, forces: the state replaces the church, philosophy supplants theology, wealth-creation becomes the most important human activity. One may hail or deplore this onset of secularization but its historical truth is not in question: it has occurred. What is of primary importance in our context is the fact, to be noted clearly, that secularization in the early modern period meant the transference, or transliteration, of erstwhile religious values and ideas into the new idiom of secular thought, and not their disappearance. The recession of Christianity *qua* revealed religion from the centre of the stage is simultaneous with its handing over its deep-structural substance – its heritage of a perspective of transcendence – to its modern successors. Changes do occur on the surface but deep below the essential message is still carried on; the new secular idiom still has an idealistic core. The operative ideas of the perspective of transcendence – the benevolent universe, objective good and evil, the elevated human species, and the exalted community – will in fact be adhered to and proclaimed more vigorously than ever before.

But of course this is not everything. It could perhaps be argued that the politicization and radicalization of Christianity in the leftwing of the Reformation and its follow-up are as it were 'logical' consequences of certain built-in tendencies of original Christian teaching and practice, simply the carrying on of a long-established tradition. But at the same time one must note that the aforementioned changes took place in the context and intellectual climate of spectacular advances in science and philosophy, and that without the latter there would (probably) not have been a radical departure in religion and politics, as described above, at all. If it is the case that the modern radical vision (including the Marxist vision) is the grandchild of secularized Christianity, it is still true that the specific *modernity* of this vision lies in its absorption of the assurances concerning the human capacity for transcendence contained in the growth of secular knowledge and understanding. In other words, the impetus comes also from outside, from the conspicuous strengthening of the other perspective imbedded in the tradition. Indeed, what is most interesting and impressive – even awe-inspiring – in the modern radical outlook is its *double* and simultaneous expression of two convictions and two perspectives: the realization of the good society is not only absolutely desirable but for the first time in the entire history of the human species it is definitely *possible*. Or, to put it more accurately (since millenarian radicals had been on the scene earlier), for the modern outlook the attainment of the ideal appears possible in historical *time*, and as the direct result of rational human *action* – as opposed to divine intervention. The Lutheran revolution proclaiming spiritual self-sufficiency must therefore be seen in the context of the Copernican revolution assigning to the earth a humble place in the universe, and therewith a seemingly modest position to the human race, one natural species among many, inhabiting one planet among many. But below the surface of humility and modesty there is the slowly gathering *hubris* of Enlightenment pride and optimism, placed in human reason the excellence and superiority of which lie precisely in *understanding* these humble and modest truths about our species and our planet. After Columbus, Copernicus and Kepler come in due course Galileo and Bacon, heralding in the great revolution in scientific method. All this culminates later, in the eighteenth century, in the mighty Newtonian system, with its universal law of gravity, directly serving as the paradigm of many a departure in radical social theorizing, including varieties of 'scientific socialism'. The idea that the growth of scientific knowledge leads logically and irreversibly to the extension of human mastery over nature, and leads also to the rational organization and control of society, is already established with Francis Bacon who writes in *The New Atlantis* (1627):

> The End of our Foundation is the knowledge of Causes, and secret motions of Things; and the enlarging of the bounds of Human Empire, to the effecting of all things possible.

Philosophy comes to emancipate itself from the domination of theology, though the first modern philosophers are still Christian believers. Descartes elevates the principle of 'doubt' as the necessary and proper starting-point of clear thinking, the sure 'method' whereby to attain to truth. Locke elaborates the doctrine of empiricism, elevating sensory experience as the only proper way in which to acquire knowledge of the natural world. With the eighteenth-century Encyclopaedists and 'materialists' (who receive a great deal of accolade from Marx and Engels in *The Holy Family*) the religious and theological shell is finally broken; war is declared on the supernatural; ignorance and superstition are to be overcome, banished from human life.

Three ideas of Enlightenment thought are deserving of special, albeit very brief, mention here. Firstly, the idea of a malleable human nature: since it is 'experience' in the world which produces the traits of human beings, new experience (coming in the wake of increasing knowledge) will create new ones; the 'human machine' is infinitely adaptable, perfectible. Secondly, the idea of progress: as history hitherto has shown how the gradual overcoming of natural obstacles produces more and more the conditions of prosperity, self-improvement and rational social organization, so this process will continue and intensify in the future. Thirdly, the idea of a purely secular, humanist morality which starts out from and remains with human 'happiness' as the greatest moral value and good to be promoted, and which on the surface at any rate contains no nonsense about 'transcendence'. One way or another, as we shall see later, and through stages of further refinement and subtle reorientation, these three ideas will act as fertile ingredients in the gestation and formation of Marxist thought.

Yet, to wind up now the story of this original 'conception' of Marxism, it would still be a grave mistake to judge the European Enlightenment to have been the *utter* routing and annihilation of the earlier tradition of transcendence, of religion and idealism. I have argued the somewhat unconventional thesis that modernity is *synthesis*, not 'fragmentation', the coming together of two opposed fundamental perspectives, *beneath* the apparent sundering of a 'unified' theological viewpoint. The latter could not have been toppled from its elevated position, had its innermost spiritual substance – the perspective of transcendence – not been salvaged and incorporated in the new outlook. Nothing essential is lost from the past. Marxism, in particular, would in my view be wholly unintelligible without our grasping this crucial point. Now it seems to me appropriate to finish this lecture by briefly referring to the philosophy of Immanuel Kant, without doubt the most outstanding thinker of the European Enlightenment, the modern equivalent of Plato. This means skipping a few stages in our story, which will be rectified in what is to follow. Kant's thought, via the intellectual mediation of German idealism and humanism, is of course important also more directly for the 'gestation' and 'formation' of Marxism, as distinguished from its original conception. But right here the significance especially of Kant's moral philosophy comes to the fore as being perhaps the most dramatic instance of the modern synthesis of the two perspectives. Kant's philosophy of the knowledge of nature is completely secular and modern, uniting Cartesian rationalism and Lockean empiricism. Our knowledge of the external world of 'phenomena', in Kant's view, comes from the experience of the senses as organized, made intelligible by the categories of human reason itself. There is no transcendence here, no penetration to 'things-in-themselves', i.e. to a reality lying *beyond* human experience and reason.

However, for Kant the world of 'practical reason' or morality is radically different. Here the human being is creator and legislator, partaking of a *real*, as distinguished from a merely 'phenomenal', world. Neither revelation nor nature but human *reason* is the fountain-head of morality, the source of our comprehending good and evil, the author of the universal and 'categorical imperative' which prescribes right conduct. The moral law of reason enjoins human beings to observe what in substance are biblical commands clad in the modern secular idiom. This law proclaims the fundamental equality of rational moral agents, to be treated as 'ends in themselves'. It is in moral conduct, following the law of reason *only*, as opposed to natural inclinations and in disregard of practical consequences, that we achieve true *freedom*, and it is only on this moral and rational foundation that human culture and civilization can flourish; we are now able, so Kant hopes, to look forward confidently to a future of 'perpetual peace'. Thus it is, in Kantian philosophy, that the ideas of transcendence and salvation of old are transliterated – salvaged – into the rational freedom of citizens living in a modern, secular society. This rational freedom, though not involving any mysterious, supernatural source, yet truly *transcends* the world of actual existence, with its conflicts, sundry desires and natural satisfactions, and moreover this rational freedom is called upon to proceed to impose its image, as far as possible, on actual existence. In the backward-looking glance we see here the chosen people of the righteous, the sublime morality of the Platonic guardians, the Gospel teaching about treating our neighbours as ourselves, the Reformation emphasis on virtue, self-sufficiency and good works, all dissolved and distilled in a mighty philosophical perspective which yet confines reality to reason and nature! And in the forward-looking glance we can observe here the gradual coming into being of the essential modern core of the Marxist enterprise which takes this idea of rational freedom as its absolute departure and sets out to realize a human 'kingdom of ends' in the three dimensions of *nature*, *society* and the *mind*. Marxist thought is already conceived: the more detailed story of its subsequent gestation, formation and bearing fruit can now be embarked upon.

GESTATION

The use of obstetric metaphors in the conceptual framework of these lectures is not as frivolous as it might seem at first. In adopting them I was led by more than rhetorical or didactic considerations. It happens to be my view that – for reasons which it would be too lengthy and digressive to elaborate here – the history of political ideas does eminently lend itself to a treatment in these terms: ideas are conceived, formed, they grow to maturity and to senility, and then they die; they can also be miscarried, aborted or malformed. In particular, so it has seemed to me, does Marxism reveal its most interesting features – its essential character, if you like – if approached thus genetically. Hence the relevance and justification of the long story of its 'conception', just concluded. Now the reason why I am calling attention to my chosen framework here – at the beginning of the second lecture, instead of the first one – is that the topic to be entered into presently, entitled the 'gestation' of Marxism, is being approached in a specially *reinforced* sense of 'obstetricism'. To wit, the point I am above all anxious to convey here is that the first phase of the growth of that which will eventually see the light of day as the thought of Marx is originally *concealed* from view, just as the embryo is concealed, invisible within the maternal womb. Moreover, the 'embryo' in this case is not only covered, hidden, lurking in the dark, but in fact externally appears as its own opposite. Marxism, in other words, gestates in the living body of our mainstream tradition in a shape which is at first hardly recognizable. It is, later, 'formed' out of a substance which to begin with has little resemblance to the end-product; in appearance (but of course in appearance only) the two negate, contradict each other, as the egg 'contradicts' the chicken and the acorn 'denies' the oaktree. And if pedants and purists were to object to this particular imagery, the presentation

44

can very easily be turned round, without forfeiting the substance of the argument. Let us say then that Marxism comes on the scene as the conscious, intended *refutation* of a doctrine which, however, *shares* its fundamental values. And looked at from the point of view of this doctrine itself: the mainstream in modern European social and political thought receives its completion, its extreme and most explicit logical conclusion, in Marxism.

What do we mean, then, by this doctrine of the modern mainstream, figuring centrally in the story of the gestation of Marxist thought? I believe I will be justified in calling it the doctrine of *European liberalism*, although the use of the word 'liberal' is somewhat anachronistic in the context. Besides, present-day usage in the 'marketplace' tends often to be restricted, applying the tag to certain narrowly defined party dogmas. On this practical level, of course, and with good reasons, Marxists and liberals regard one another as bitter antagonists. But this still does not change the historical and conceptual truth that Marxism did grow out of liberalism, assuming and adapting the values and overall perspective of liberalism, and that without this broad liberal background Marxism would be unimaginable and non-existent. It is to avoid question-begging that I am using the term, liberalism, instead of that which might both sound more familiar to Marxists and at the same time express the point I am making more clearly and succinctly. That is to say, by liberalism here I mean no less and no more than what Marx and Engels themselves designated in scores of places as the intellectual substance of 'bourgeois ideology' befitting the class of the bourgeoisie – and this is a very important modification – during the *progressive* phase of its historical presence. As the bourgeois class, so runs this pivotal Marxist argument, consolidates its position in society as the holder of power, generates its antagonist and eventual grave-digger, the modern industrial proletariat, and consequently ceases to be 'progressive' (in terms of material productivity, etc.), so its prevailing mainstream ideology, liberalism, also begins to sound *hollow*, ready to be surpassed and refuted. But, in Marx's terms the proletariat now turns the bourgeoisie's 'own weapons' against the bourgeoisie, and this applies also on the ideological level: the very progressive core of bourgeois thought is now developed further, becomes the perspective of the proletariat *now* representing historical 'progress', and actively employed in the struggle to end capitalist domination.

Thus European liberal thought is broadly speaking equivalent to what we called in the previous lecture the *modern synthesis*. It represents the paradigmatic outlook of modernity in the field of social and political theorizing, the 'conventional wisdom' of the age, a rich family of values and organizing concepts which it may be difficult to identify only on account of its very familiarity. Liberalism in this epochal, generic sense is what has been (and still is, to a large extent) taken for granted in European political theory, the very foundations and also broad aims of what are regarded as good government and desirable social relations. The liberal paradigm, of which we have already had a momentary glimpse in the foregoing, begins to take shape in the age of Renaissance and Reformation, fuelled by the advancement in science and philosophy, given spur by geographical discoveries and the expansion of European power (military, economic, cultural) all over the globe. Victorious first in the Netherlands and England with the Civil War and the Glorious Revolution, its dizziest climax as a *Weltanschauung* comes with the American War of Independence and the great French Revolution, and gets enshrined in venerable constitutional declarations and inspired tracts and treatises – this is the heroic age of modern political theory. Liberalism achieves its greatest practical (as distinguished from theoretical) triumphs in the mid-nineteenth century, in a series of revolutions and changes in the political and social structure of European states; already, however, with the onset of nationalism and economic 'protection', theoretically speaking it begins now slowly to move over to the defensive. Its last great stand, as the dominant progressive paradigm of the age, is with the Wilsonian crusade for 'self-determination', after the world was made 'safe for democracy'. We all know how that ended up. The vigorous 'neo-liberalism' of our own times, of course, is avowedly *conservative*, i.e. consciously harking back to the heroic foundations, a force for political and social consolidation.

The family of liberal values and ideas is rich, extensive and complex. It is certainly not an irresponsible or superficial sleight of hand to connect liberalism with 'democracy', since in the modern age democracy *is*, very largely, derived from and remains closely connected to basic liberal values, such as individual rights, freedom of activity, legality, constitutional guarantees, limited government. Liberalism shades into, elicits, democracy at least in the areas of law and politics, moving (or being pushed) towards further extensions of the scope and rights of the 'individual'. Liberalism – obviously – centres on the notion of individual freedom, on the unhampered, unconstrained expansion of powers and potentials flowing from individuals in their actual existence (the basic liberal value which, by the way, receives its highest accolade in *The Communist Manifesto* – not that we are trying here to establish *glib* correspondences). Individual freedom in the classical liberal perspective is both an aim and a basic condition of life: individuals are in the last resort 'alone' in society, equally vulnerable to encroachment by other individuals and morally equal in endeavouring to protect themselves and 'do their own thing'. Power, therefore, in the liberal view has to be circumscribed and restrained; hence the liberal emphasis on the need to define the scope of government clearly and rather narrowly, in terms of individual 'rights' enshrined in legislation and safeguarded by the actual dispersion of power: hence social 'pluralism', countervailing powers, the separation of offices, the 'toleration' of diverse opinions and the protection of 'privacy'. Hence also, which is the logical extension of liberalism, the 'democratic' control over governmental power by institutionalized procedures, like individual franchise and periodic elections. Societal authority, to put it in one phrase, in the liberal perspective flows *upwards*, from individuals comprising the 'people'. Now just to project forward to our discussion later on: as we shall see, in Marxism also there is an unreserved, enthusiastic acceptance of individual freedom as a supreme aim and value; where liberalism is resolutely rejected (or 'constructively developed') is only on the lower levels, i.e. concerning individual freedom as a *basic condition* of life and concerning the nature of *actual power* in society.

For now, however, it will be necessary for us to attempt to create some sort of order and intelligibility among basic liberal concepts and values. I propose, with a view to presenting European liberalism as the 'gestation period' of Marxism, to divide the liberal perspective schematically into three avenues or dimensions; this division, it seems to me, is not only suitable for the purpose at hand but also commonsensical, suggested by the subject matter itself, and in broad conformity with accustomed academic procedures. That is to say, let us establish that this basic liberal paradigm contains a *political* idea, a *social* idea and a *philosophical* idea. They all, in different ways, concern themselves with illuminating the relationship (both actual and desirable) among single individuals and of the single individual to 'society' in general. By the political idea of liberalism I am referring to the view that rational individual human beings are 'autonomous' in their perception of right and wrong, are equal in their moral capacity and moral responsibility, and that therefore *formally* at least they have an equal claim to participate in – or at the minimum influence and sanction – the structures and processes of government. In short, and as it came to be expressed in terms of the paradigm, individuals have equal 'natural rights' in society. By the social idea of liberalism I mean the con-sequential (and it *is* consequential) notion that individuals are the best judges of their own capacities and interests, and therefore ought to be allowed, as far as possible, to create the conditions of their own individual 'happiness' in their diverse ways. Moral and basic political equality, in other words, gives rise to, 'liber-ates' as it were, an abundance of substantive diversities, 'social' inequalities, and this outcome in the liberal view is highly desirable, conducive to general happiness. In short, this is the idea of 'free enterprise'. Thirdly, by the philosophical idea of liberalism I am referring here to the venerable efforts made by a number of philosophers to reconcile and unify the political and social values involved in liberalism – it is not difficult to see that there is a tension between the two. This effort has typically been made in terms of elaborate definitions of the 'state' as moral community and a source of moral uplift, and the 'law' of the state as emanating from the 'will' of individuals. I do not need to emphasize the fact that these three ideas have been closely intertwined in the actual, historical existence of liberal thought, with writers subscribing to all three but with differing emphases.

It is these three fundamental ideas of European liberalism which, as we shall have the opportunity to see in the next lecture, will seemingly undergo a process of metamorphosis and come to view as the root ideas of the three – decidedly non-liberal! – departures in modern radicalism directly involved in the actual, and *visible* this time, 'formation' of Marxist thought. The idea of the socialist or communist organization of society springs from the idea of equal natural rights – there is no question concerning the logic, the pedigree, the actual derivation. The idea of critical social science – socialist political economy – grows out of the notion of free individual enterprise. Here the derivation, admittedly, is not so obvious but – by the same token – all the more interesting for us to uncover. And the idea of revolutionary humanism has its source and base in the soaring thought of liberalism in attempting to reconcile political equality and social freedom in the modern state. But socialist theory *has* to be democratic theory first, socialist economy must presuppose liberal economy, and modern humanism has no meaning except as the outgrowth of idealist philosophy. Otherwise these radical departures would lack not only their historical *raison d'être* but also their logical starting-point, their first major premise. In political argument it is not possible to deny everything asserted by your antagonist; what happens is that you critically resolve and modify something from the opponent's thesis on the basis of assuming and accepting something else, shared between you. In this case, in the movement from liberalism to modern political radicalism, the assumption and acceptance concern the fundamentals – moral equality, free activity, soaring thought – and critical rejection and modification concern their secondary derivatives and their particular application only, what socialists were to assert later was the 'betrayal' by the bourgeoisie of the heritage of the Enlightenment, the *arrest* of the development of liberal ideas at the hands of liberals themselves.

This is a convenient place to reiterate the main point made in the closing section of the previous lecture but now with added and timely emphasis. The perspective of European liberalism, projectively viewed, is the harbinger of modern European social-ism and communism. Retrospectively viewed it is the synthesis of our original traditions of (religious) transcendence and (scientific) understanding, and liberalism passes on this synthesis to its successors, Marxism in particular. The three basic ideas of liberal thought presuppose and are based on the synthesis; they are ideas of transcendence informed and validated by understanding. In the modern ideas of equality, freedom and their reconciliation in the state (the 'soaring thought' of liberalism) we find deeply imbedded the ideas of the benevolent universe, objective good and evil, the elevation of the species, and the value of the community; and just as firmly are these ideas based on the original 'cool looks' at nature, society and human values. The liberal and later the socialist vista involve a *good society consisting of happy individuals*. The extent to which we as contemporary observers tend *not* to question the harmony and compatibility of general goodness and individual happiness clearly demonstrates our being deeply in thrall to modernity, a consciousness which can be loosened – and this, I take it, is what academc education in this field, in the humanities in general, is all about – only by becoming acquainted with the *whole* story. Nowhere, to repeat, is this exercise of loosening more warranted than in a study of the genesis of Marxism; here this is the best way in which to become appreciative of (intellectual) beauties as well as blemishes. The point to be made therefore, repeatedly, is that in inheriting the synthesis of modernity – from liberalism to socialism – Marxism also inherits its underlying *problems*.

The last general remark I would like to make, before entering into a more detailed discussion, is that the sequential unfolding of the three basic ideas of liberalism is broadly speaking an *historical fact*, discounting minor discrepancies, not invented by Marx nor by me just in order to be able to present this lecture. What I have called the political idea of liberalism is dominant first, then comes the social, and finally the philosophical idea. In 'secular' history this is underlined by the sequence of such key and decisive events as the French Revolution, the Repeal of the Corn Laws in England, and the consolidation of constitutional monarchies and parliamentary republics in Europe. Perhaps one should not (unless one is prepared to encounter a charge of 'vulgar' Marxism) make too much of this: we are referring here to a *broad trend*, not to a perfect and exhaustive sequence of events. But at least on the level of ideas – which is our principal concern here – the sequence is certainly intelligible and necessary to keep in mind. To put it succinctly but I hope not too crudely: it is equal natural rights which raised the problem of individual freedom which in turn raises the problem of having to reconcile this freedom with equality. What are morally equal individuals *to do*, once their common arena of activities is established? And what if their activities in practice become *harmful* to equality, individual 'freedom' leading to the *skewed* distribution of power in this common arena of society? And so on. This, in a nutshell, is what we might call the fundamental dilemma of modern political and social theory, *centrally* concerning liberal theory and practice but also afflict-ing the latter-day practice – as distinguished from the high theory – of Marxism. If there is any conclusion to be drawn from this discrepancy (and strictly speaking Marxist 'practice' is not a part of the story of the genesis of Marxism), the proper place for it will be later on.

*   *   *

The doctrine of equal *natural rights* charts a sequence of deri-vation from liberalism to Marxism which is neat and robust, indeed frightening in its very simplicity and revolutionary momentum. This political underpinning of the liberal per-spective has of course been more prominent on the 'leftwing' of the historical movement but by no means confined to it. The 'logic' of equal natural rights leads necessarily from radical democracy to revolutionary communism. The development is punctuated by the crystallization of the idea of the 'sovereign people', i.e. the collective essence of morally equal, free and rational individuals, first, and then by the effective criticism of actual conditions which appear to prevent popular sovereignity from becoming substantive reality. That is to say, believers in natural rights note that social inequalities make a mockery of moral equality, and that the cause and mainstay of these inequalities is the maldistribution of property and wealth, result-ing in power being used to oppress and exploit the poor. Hence comes the demand for the equal distribution of property, which is only one (and not too long) step away from the socialization of property, i.e. socialism. But equalization must be brought about against the wishes and interests of those at present holding wealth and consequent political power. Hence the justification and need for revolution: true equality can only arrive after the violent overthrow of the group of individuals now ruling. But, further, those now ruling can exercise their oppressive social power only by successfully *misleading* the poor as to the latter's position and interest; the oppressed, therefore, are themselves actively contributing to their own oppression. Hence, finally, the need for a temporary 'educational dictatorship' by a minority of clearsighted and purposeful revolutionaries. Thus the logical sequence, stated here in bare summary terms. In this lecture I shall proceed only to the step of the criticism of unequal wealth – the rest belongs to socialism proper, not to liberalism. Instead of following this egalitarian logic through, I shall take the *sideways* step of commenting, in the next section of the present lecture, on the 'social' idea of liberalism. It is remarkable, to digress now for a moment, that although the logic of radical democracy is *unquestionably* a constituent part of the modern foundations of Marxism, its importance is usually played down in Marxist commentaries (and by Marx himself). Perhaps to some extent this is a result of this tradition being so stark, so robust, so frightening.

Of the idea of 'natural right' in the first place we ought to note, of course, that it derives from the Christian (and ultimately Stoic) notion of a 'law of nature', governing, among other things, moral conduct by and among human beings. The characteristically modern stance on natural law is one that gradually shifts the focus on to individuals abstracted from social relations whose 'natural right' is logically prior to the establishment of government and the incurring of specific individual duties and obligations. The effect of the Reformation, with its doctrine of 'individual priesthood', on this development is unmistakable, and from Grotius and Hobbes onwards, culminating in the doctrines of Locke, Pufendorf and Spinoza, the operative paradigm of political theory is the 'social contract', connecting individuals in their abstracted 'natural state' to existing structures the legitimacy of which is derived from the 'contract'. The radical – even revolutionary – implications of this individualism begin to surface only later, however, after the waning of Protestant doctrinal influence and the triumph of the Enlightenment. Stressing individual reason and at the same time natural sociability, this modern doctrine of natural right takes on an egalitarian and democratic edge which will, eventually, push it in the direction of socialism and communism.

We can briefly illustrate the first stage of this radical development by reference to the ideas of Jean-Jacques Rousseau, the most influential advocate of popular sovereignty in the period. Though, again, not being one of Marx's greatest heroes and not himself being drawn to explicit socialist conclusions (as were some of his contemporaries, Morelly for example), Rousseau is most important in our discussion, since his writings clearly exhibit the tension and dynamism implicit in liberal thinking. (Marx read and digested Rousseau, it appears, during his honeymoon in Kreuznach.) Rousseau is the liberal thinker who moves *directly* from radical individualism to democratic collectivism, from equal natural right to the idea of the sovereign people; and besides, his *critique* of eighteenth century 'civilized' society (with its inegalitarian features, aristocratic privileges, autocratic government, etc.) contain elements very conspicuous in subsequent socialist texts (right down, we might add, to the documents of the 'New Left' in the 1960s).

Rousseau's explosive essay on the 'Origin of Inequality' (1754), for example, postulates the 'natural' human being, before and without the corruption of civilized society, as an inherently sociable creature, with the only two basic traits of self-regard and compassion, i.e. fellow-feeling for other humans. In Rousseau's hypostatized 'natural state' physical inequalities have no significance whatever, as individuals are mindful only of their moral equality. The strong here has no reason to impose his power on the weak; all are free and independent in their natural sociability, living in 'loose associations'. Corruption sets in, however, as a result of two parallel historical processes, one external and concerning economic development (agriculture, industry, trade), the other internal and marking the degradation of individual consciousness from independent sociability to competitive egoism. Albeit thus operating with a 'semi-materialist' conception of history (if a more direct link to Marx were to be sought), Rousseau puts the emphasis on the latter process: the change from 'self-regard' to 'self-love', played out in comparing oneself to others and in wanting to excel over others, is what ultimately causes oppression and exploitation in civilized society. Only egoistic and slave-minded individuals, preferring their 'private' gains to their shared humanity, can be oppressed and be induced to acquiesce in drastic inequalities of power and wealth. The rich and strong from then on can impose their rule over the poor and wretched, with naked group-interest now masquerading as law and authority. Rousseau's conclusion is bitter and hard:

> Such was, or may well have been, the origin of society and law, which bound new fetters on the poor, and gave new powers to the rich; which irretrievably destroyed natural liberty, eternally fixed the law of property and inequality, converted clever usurpation into unalterable right, and, for the advantage of a few ambitious individuals, subjected all mankind to perpetual labour, slavery and wretchedness.

Indeed, while Rousseau's socialism is only embryonic (if that) and the materialism in his view of historical progression is subdued, there is displayed another element in his critique of inequality and civilization which especially today would be seen as being quite significant in the genesis of Marxism. This concerns Rousseau's heavy emphasis on the inauthenticity and other-directedness of individual consciousness in civilized society; human beings, as Rousseau appears to argue, are not quite themselves in actual existence, not what they could and should be in ideal conditions, what they *essentially* are, in their original 'natural' state. Note here the synthesis of the perspectives of transcendence and understanding: Rousseau directly derives the human ideal from human *nature*. And note also, projecting forward, the central relevance of Rousseau's concept of inauthenticity to the concept of 'estrangement' or 'alienation' as appearing in Marx's early texts. Marx's concept, as we shall see in due course, is much richer and more penetrating than Rousseau's; however, the Rousseauist critique of culture and civilization – which, in a way, is a profound internal *self*-critique of modernity – is undoubtedly one of its chief sources, its 'idealist' leg as it were (the other, 'materialist', leg, comes from liberal political economy, as we shall observe in a minute).

It is not just Rousseau's critique, however, that has to be adduced here but also Rousseau's proffered solution to the maladies of modern alienation and equality. This solution, it can be argued, is in fact more important than Rousseau's critique in establishing the perspective of radical democracy which will lead, via revolutionary communism, to the doctrine of Marxism. Rousseau's solution is the state – the legally constituted community – which embodies the sovereignty of the people and the 'general will' of assembled rational amd morally equal individuals. In his epoch-making treatise, *The Social Contract*, Rousseau declares the 'general will' of the people to be the only legitimate source of power and authority in the state. It is only this way, through self-government, that individuals can recreate their 'original' freedom, dignity and sociability. In this community individual natural right is not lost but sublimated, transfigured, enriched in moral content; the *authentic* 'will' of the individual it is that promotes the *general* good of all individuals in the state. Only by totally giving themselves up or 'alienating' their individual selves to the community can people regain their *natural* individual selves and thus safeguard against the partial – and damaging – self-alienation which produces inequality and oppression. In Rousseau's terms it is perfectly consistent to contend that individuals are 'forced to be free' by the authority of the general will; it is their own, moral as well as natural, will which is pitted against their private and 'particular' volition, the latter being merely an historically contingent surface result of the corrupting influence of civilized society.

It could be argued that while Rousseau's scenario is too stark, too radical and too simplistic in terms of its basic principle, it does not go far enough in terms of following and spelling out the practical implications. The principle involved is one of uncompromising, extreme egalitarianism, postulating the *total* and palpable convergence of individual, group and societal aims and interests; hence the somewhat tendentious tag, 'totalitarian democracy' (of which an influential modern school of interpretation pronounces Rousseau to be one of the 'founders') is not entirely misplaced. However, there is no cause to read anything particularly nasty and sinister into Rousseau. Rather what is of chief interest here is the concealed and disturbing *disjunction* in Rousseau's political thought. Radical political equality requires, it might be assumed, a very considerable dose of substantive equality, or equality of social and economic conditions. The supposed common moral interest of individuals can have practical significance only if it is matched by the harmony of their material interest, and this harmony would not be forthcoming in conditions of extreme inequality and built-in particular privileges. Of course to some extent Rousseau is aware of this, and there are numerous well-intentioned, though vague and inconclusive, references to the desirability of equalizing wealth in the pages of *The Social Contract* and elsewhere in his writings. But by and large Rousseau leaves a gap between state and society, or between the bare, abstract principle of the general will (which is radical and egalitarian) and its *actual* operation; the latter, as one learns from reading subsequent chapters of Rousseau's great treatise, is very far from being seen by Rousseau in 'totalitarian' terms. There are in fact two directions implicit in Rousseau's doctrine of popular sovereignty. One, taken up by the radical wing of the French Revolution and issuing in revolutionary communism (which we will survey in the next lecture), proceeds by taking substantive equality seriously and moving from the 'equalization' to the 'socialization' of wealth and property. The other, leaving us still on the plane of mainstream liberalism, proceeds as it were by relegating the principle of equality 'upstairs', rendering it to some extent innocuous (though by no means false or meaningless) as merely a *preamble* to actual laws, governmental structures, and group and individual relations in society. In the latter case, in the mainstream development of liberalism (and issuing in 'liberal democracy'), the moral totality of the community is *remotely* and *inversely* reflected in an arena of diverging particular interests. Individual consciousness and existence *in society*, in other words, overshadows the moral equality and convergence of individuals as existing – in principle – in the state.

*   *   *

It is at this point that we shall leave – for the time being – the tradition of radical democracy behind and turn to what I have called earlier the *social* idea of liberalism. It is not to be imagined for a moment – though the foregoing paragraph may have suggested this – that this idea has merely or even essentially, a negative significance in and for the gestation of Marxism, that is, an idea to be combated, refuted, overcome. The situation is by no means so simple; indeed, with a modest amount of didactic exaggeration, we might want here to argue that the liberal tradition epitomized under this 'social' label is *more* important for Marxism than the tradition of radical democracy. It is if we view Marx in the context of fellow socialists and communists, as distinguished from the wider and deeper historical context of eminent mainstream Western political thinkers, that the paramount importance of the liberal perspective on society comes to the fore; it is from this source, and not from radical democracy, that Marx derives his science of political economy, representing the one area of intellectual achievement to his lasting credit. Here perhaps we should once more draw explicit attention to the fascinating duality of Marx's thought (in which the duality of our whole tradition is telescoped), occupying the idealistic world of revolution as well as the realistic world of social science. If Marxism has one *wild* parent in the tradition of egalitarian democracy, it also has an eminently *respectable* parent in the tradition of liberal political economy. I suppose in the last resort it is a matter of individual taste and preference which 'parent' of the two is pronounced more important, more deserving; mine has been indicated already in this paragraph.

There is nothing new or specifically modern in the idea of a 'science' of human institutions and relationships; this goes back, as we saw in the first lecture, at least to the time of Aristotle. What is new and modern, however, is the subject matter of this science, viz. 'society'. Modern political thought identifies the *state* first, as an autonomous body of 'law and order', authority and power concentrated. It is only afterwards and on the assumption of this legal order, that thinkers begin to pay increasing attention to the 'actual existence' of states, endeavouring to find out both what is going on within the framework of legality and what should be going on. Thus *society* – a field of interaction among individuals – takes definite shape also as a proper object of study, with its own laws, patterns, regularities. It is important to note that the constituent elements of modern society are 'individuals', i.e. human beings defined essentially in terms of their abstract relationship to the generality of the state, and not in terms of their particular social roles and positions, as in the Middle Ages (e.g. nobles, serfs, guildsmen etc.). Of course in this developing 'bourgeois' society individuals do continue to have particular allegiances and group identities (as well as generating new ones) but nevertheless these are viewed in the new perspective of social science *as if* they were secondary to 'individual' background, motivation, action and interest.

The perspective here described obviously corresponds to a *new way of life*, developing in Western Europe, based mainly on cities and seaports, the way of life of traders, merchants, bankers and later manufacturers. Their activity is formally 'independent' and also in a sense adventurous: the outcome of entrepreneurial actions is in principle always uncertain. Hence the new 'freedom' involved in commercial activity requires the provision of general security, protection by the state. Free private property thrives and expands under the umbrella of public authority. Society, therefore, although chaotic and shapeless from the individual point of view (for enterprising individuals it is essentially an 'arena' for private action), does have a recognizable shape if viewed from 'above' or 'outside', by the scientific observer whose perspective is detached and 'objective'. Individual actions display regular patterns in the aggregate; these can be classified, cross-related, to a large extent they are predictable. Society is like nature; needless to say, this new emerging social scientific perspective as part of the liberal paradigm receives a tremendous boost also from modern advances in natural science and in philosophy, referred to earlier. In time the domain of social science will come to embrace practically everything to do with human life – and the impact of Marxism itself is of course very considerable in this process – including such branches as literary sociology, social psychology, mathematical history.

But it all begins with 'political economy', the original model for social science (and still today its basis and fulcrum). Society in the first and basic instance is the field of interaction among individuals engaged in the activity of *wealth-creation*. This is the area where – whatever happens in other areas – the 'units' interacting do show consistency and regularity over time and in space. This is where the human species, in a manner of speaking, actively relates to nature, the world outside, containing lower and simpler forms of life, and nature is waiting and indeed asking for itself to be used for human ends. The complexities and varieties of economic organization thus reduce themselves to these two simple principles: firstly, in economic activity human beings deal with nature in a direct and positive way, exploiting it and transforming it, and secondly they do this in order to enhance their own natural existence, acting in the social aggregate but on the basis of conscious individual motivation. Thus on the one hand the production, distribution and exchange of consumable goods ('wealth' for short) are in principle amenable to scientific study – as the 'partner' in economic activity, nature, is also a proper object of understanding. And on the other hand it is precisely in economic activity that the complex character of human beings (consciousness, motivation, emotions, morality, etc.) is legitimately reduced to a basic human 'nature', the robust, simple, crude and if you like *vulgar* nature of the wealth-maker and wealth-gatherer. The prototype of the modern 'rational person' is so-called 'economic man' whose rationality is instrumental, whose principal activity is wealth-creation, and whose human and social relationships tend also to conform to this economic pattern.

'Economic man' wants to live well, amply, in conditions of comfort. In order to consume he must produce, use his individual powers in the arena of society or the 'market' where individuals come into contact as *exchangers*, impersonally and using one another as the 'means' to the gaining of private individual ends. The market, as the basic model of the 'society' studied by political economists, is not like the *agora* of the ancient city-state where people met as participants in a common discussion, people as *personally* related, friends or enemies – the model, incidentally, for the Rousseauist radical democratic scenario for the playing out of the 'general will'. In the latter there is an achieved unity of individual wills, whereas in the modern market where participants are *abstractly* related, individual wills are not united but instead seen as *complementary*, confirmed as private but mutually dovetailing. All individuals are in principle economic self-seekers and it is as such – hopefully – that they will manage to harmonize their interests and maintain their social interaction.

Here we have to note a point of considerable importance for the study of the genesis of Marxism and alas this point is not always sufficiently appreciated. What we need to grasp clearly is that this *social* idea of liberalism – as epitomized in the perspective of classical political economy – strikes a markedly more *modern* note than the political idea of liberalism we have seen formulated in terms of popular sovereignty and radical democracy. The latter idea is, no doubt, strident, subversive, revolutionary – on the surface and in respect of its short-term practical implications. But at bottom it is still essentially our old perspective of transcendence, merely transposed into a modern idiom. It's 'coolness' is mainly in the language used, and not always in that either; its general tendency is to exhort, to moralize, and it simply reads the ideal into some selected features of actual existence. Political economy, by contrast, presents an immediate appearance of staidness, dullness, accommodation, unexciting conservatism, the crude commonsense, indeed, of the 'marketplace'; but nevertheless its underlying principle is radical and modern. It is not liberal politics but liberal society which is really the watershed between the old and the new, the decisive break (in so far as there is one) with accustomed ways of thinking and acting which up to then retarded the full flowering of the modern European spirit. With liberal political economy what counts is where it starts from, and not where it stops. It starts from the individual being, man the producer confronting nature, creating the conditions of worldly human happiness. It stops – stops short, looked at from the socialist point of view – with production organized around free individual and 'private' enterprise; socialists will go much further but they will proceed from the same starting-point. And in so far, unlike radical democracy, as the liberal social idea is squarely rooted in the experience of actual existence, its *language*, the idiom of unadorned, unashamed, everyday 'reality', becomes the language of incipient social science – the deadpan, dispassionate, detached, fact-oriented, 'value-free' language of classical political economy, inherited, developed and displayed to good effect in Marx's science of capital.

The origins of political economy (once again) go back to the Greeks for whom, however, and also for medieval Christian writers, the importance of livelihood concerns – production, trade, affairs of the household, etc. – is secondary to 'public' matters, like statecraft, culture and religious worship. From being regarded as vulgar and trivial, even sinful, the activity and values of wealth-creation begin to receive increased attention and indeed enthusiastic recognition as the modern age emerges, attendant on the liberation of the 'individual' in his own actual milieu, the 'society' of self-regarding and economically interacting individuals. An important landmark here is Locke's *Second Treatise of Civil Government* (1688) – one of those notorious 'bibles of the bourgeoisie', in Marxist parlance – where we find three key ideas of modern liberalism already clearly formulated. One is the idea of 'civil society', i.e., a network of orderly relationships among individuals, pre-existing and justifying the institution of government. The second one is the concept of 'labour' which in Locke's wide and vague definition refers to individual enterprise in general. It is 'labour' alone, as Locke forcefully argues, that gives the original title to the products of nature. The third is the idea of 'private property', that is, products or resources of nature owned by single individuals exclusively, based on their 'labour' performed in 'civil society'. Thus the 'society' of producing and property-owning individuals is *read into* nature, this is what is good, what is original, what is just. The rest, i.e. government, legislation, jurisdiction, foreign relations, etc. are secondary, artificially created for the protection and convenience of society. Locke has no 'science' of political economy as such but what appears later bearing this designation is unmistakably built on these basic assumptions and concepts.

Another important landmark in the emergence of the social idea of liberalism can be located in Montesquieu's epoch-making (though today, compared to Locke or Rousseau, rather archaic-sounding) treatise, *The Spirit of the Laws* (1748). What this lengthy book is especially famous for, of course, is its doctrine of the 'separation of the powers', later to become an absolute first principle of the liberal theory of government (and one which is entirely consistent with the idea of a society of privately producing and owning individuals). But in the present context two other things found in Montesquieu deserve a brief mention, as being significant elements in the emerging body of modern political economy. One is Montesquieu's strong emphasis on the influence of the natural environment on the character of individuals, states, governments, social relations. Historical determination, in other words, is 'from below', from nature and not from an active divine providence – the view represented by Montesquieu is a kind of antediluvian 'historical materialism', if you like, entering into the doctrine of the classical political economists later and from there into Marxism. Secondly and more specifically, Montesquieu tends to look upon history as *economic* history, i.e. judging the manner of earning their livelihood as being basic to the definition of various types of society. Human history, as he argues in Book XVIII of *The Spirit of the Laws*, moves from savagery through barbarism and agriculture to commerce, with the use of money being the most important sign of civilization and culture. Adam Smith's famous 'four stages' theory of historical development is said to have been inspired by this view of Montesquieu's. Yet another significant departure is found in the French Physiocratic writers, notably Quesnay and Mirabeau (father of the famous revolutionary leader), with whom arguably political economy first begins to assume a proper scientific character. Attention with these writers is focused on the system of production, distribution and exchange, and the constituent 'orders' of society are defined by them in terms of their function in the economic system. The most famous Physiocrat, Turgot, was Adam Smith's contemporary and a leading French statesman in the reign of Louis XVI, noted for his early 'liberal' advocacy of taxation for the nobility and the abolition of commercial privileges. Smith knew and was influenced by the Physiocrats, chiefly Turgot whose great work, *Reflections on the Formation and Distribution of Wealth*, preceded the appearance of the former's own renowned treatise, which is without question *the* definitive text of classical political economy.

Readers will, I hope, forgive what might seem a disproportionate amount of time to be devoted here to Smith's gigantic *Inquiry into the Nature and Causes of the Wealth of Nations* (1776), and for the occasional hyperbola in presenting its principal ideas. As single 'texts' go, I think it is beyond dispute that the *Wealth of Nations* is one of the two most important pieces figuring in the history of the genesis of Marxism, and more particularly of its half-concealed 'gestation' in the thought of modern liberalism (the other being Hegel's *Phenomenology* which, however, will receive a more curtailed treatment – for reasons which I will explain later). Marx in his formative years, as we shall see in due course, not only receives and absorbs the main ideas of liberal political economy as a kind of 'revelation' but also adopts and repeats so many of Smith's detailed formulations and concrete examples as to make it almost embarrassing for the reader who – moving from Marx's texts back to his predecessors, which is probably the way followed by most students of Marxism – at first placed Marx's 'originality' on a much higher level. Besides, the *Wealth of Nations* is an extremely readable book, serious and concentrated but at the same time clear, concise and devoid of dense logical obscurities (which its great successor, Marx's *Capital*, is unfortunately not), judiciously and pleasantly combining scientific generalization, historical commentary, empirical detail and dry 'social comment'. Regarding the last, it has to be said that although Smith's viewpoint is that of mainstream liberalism – his view is, indeed, one of the enduring paradigms *within* liberal political and social thinking – he is not a simple-minded and onesided apologist of capitalism and bourgeois class society. Liberal social science at this stage does embody a 'cool look' in the specific sense of academic detachment which involves advocacy as well as criticism. I would like to quote an apt remark here from Duncan Forbes' Introduction (1966) to *An Essay on the History of Civil Society* (1767) by Adam Ferguson, one of the other illustrious representatives of the great Scottish Enlightenment:

Not only Ferguson but Smith and Millar too, and others
... took a *long, cool look* at both sides of the medal of
modern civilization, and what they saw was the paradox
of the progress of commerce and manufactures giving rise
on the one hand to personal liberty and security, the
blessings of the rule of law, but at the same time and
equally inevitably producing a second-rate sort of society
full of second-rate citizens pursuing comparatively
worthless objects. Smith's nineteenth-century critics and
admirers both failed to appreciate the penetration and
force of his criticism of that type of civilization which he
appeared to be advocating, and which indeed he *was*
advocating.

The Wealth of Nations, if one should venture a terse
summary, contains two basic ideas on which Smith builds his
science. The first is what we might call Smith's basic factual or
empirical premise, the view that he takes of 'actual existence'.
This view is that there is a 'natural' human being who inhabits
a 'natural' human society. 'Natural' refers here not to what was
supposed to have been going on some time in a remote past
(as in Locke's 'natural state') or among innocent savages, and
lamentably absent from 'civilization' (as in Rousseau), but what
is going on now, *in* civilization, the bottom layer as it were of
actual human conduct and social transactions. The natural
human being produces, consumes and exchanges in the market –
'natural' human society – to his own benefit. The rest (practically) of what is found in actual social existence is for Smith
artificial, i.e. all kinds of conventions and institutions (like the
state) which may be beneficial or harmful to natural man and
society. The point is that for Smith artificial arrangements can
and should be rationally understood, and altered if necessary,
whereas one cannot so easily (and certainly should not try to)
tamper with nature. This distinction, it seems to me, prefigures
in a significant way the later Marxist distinction between 'base'
and 'superstructure' in the mode of production: the former, for
Marx, is what is going on 'naturally' (i.e. the 'inexorable' laws
of economic change) and is merely 'reflected' in the movement
of the latter. Of course there are important differences between

Smith and Marx, too: Smith's determinism is by no means as marked as Marx's and his *valuation* of the 'natural' is obviously rather different. But this is just a digression, not to be pursued any further here.

The second basic idea of the *Wealth of Nations* to be mentioned here is what we might term Smith's value premise, adjoining his factual premise. This is simply that it is a good thing – indeed the primary moral aim – to promote the 'natural liberty' of individuals, and this according to Smith is best achieved if the (artificial) institutional structure of society is reduced to a judicious minimum, which goes with the recognition of its *negative* role in the pursuit of individual happiness, i.e. the provision of security, the protection of the market. 'Laissez faire, laissez passer' – here we have the famous liberal 'night-watchman' theory of the state in a nutshell. Smith's most well-known and influential argument in favour of this value premise, his great discovery as it were, is the so-called 'invisible hand': the pursuit of natural liberty by individuals seeking their own ends will 'invisibly' promote the common good or the end of all individuals. I might be putting this a little bit too crudely but this certainly seems to be the crux of the message: the morality or consciousness needed to serve the interests of the whole of society is just 'enlightened individual self-interest', and *not* another, higher kind of 'social' morality (as it is with Rousseau and the radical democrats). Individuals do act selfishly but in the aggregate their actions nevertheless have an unselfish conclusion; the unintended and by them unforeseen consequences of their actions will achieve the optimum all-round situation attainable. Reason, morality, justice, in other words, can best operate underground, *through* actual human nature; the intrusion of artificial social institutions – endeavouring, as it were, to bring reason and morality to the surface, to elevate it *above* nature, to promote the common good deliberately – has only a harmful effect. Now Smith assumes in *The Wealth of Nations* (and the arguments are outlined fully in his other seminal work, *The Theory of Moral Sentiments*) that individuals are naturally *fit* for society: their basic inclination is to conduct themselves selfishly but not in a wild, anarchistic, irresponsible way. Their makeup also naturally contains 'moral sentiments', like the inner voice of conscience and the faculty of impartiality, of seeing things objectively, from the viewpoint of the detached spectator (e.g. students of society with their scientific perspective). Further, although Smith regards basic market relations as being adequate in ensuring social justice, his vision includes a progression towards a level of consciousness higher than the existing one, towards education and culture, but of course still built on the foundations of 'natural liberty'.

Smith's outline of the system of wealth-creation in 'civilized society' (i.e. with individuals acting on their natural liberty, unlike preceding 'rude' stages of social development) contains too many details which obviously we have to skip here, fascinating though some of them might be. The essential and here relevant concepts in this account of the workings of the market are labour, the division of labour, the propensity to exchange, the determination of value, and the distribution of revenue to the various orders of society. Labour is the starting-point: in order to consume people must exert themselves, in whichever way, so as to be able to *serve* the desires, interests of others. Civilized individuals recognize themselves as the proprietors of their socially productive energy, so (unlike animals) they have a natural propensity to *exchange* the product of their individual effort for products they wish to consume (or for the means which will enhance their own productivity). But labour becomes more productive, and hence wealth-creation and consumption more plentiful, if it spreads out and becomes a multiplicity of specialized pursuits, each productive in its own narrow way, and together producing more than labour undivided. For Smith the historical progression towards increasing, and more and more articulate, *division* of labour is the key element in civilization, the guarantee of enhanced material prosperity and hence peace, security and happiness. A point of considerable importance and interest to note here is Smith's unambiguous view in regarding the division of labour as the *cause* of human inequality, and not its effect. Smith's perspective is thoroughly modern and liberal in the way in which this term was defined here earlier: the natural moral equality of human beings is just as much his starting-point as it is Rousseau's. The *political* idea of liberalism, as we have argued earlier, logically precedes its *social* idea. But furthermore, in his more concentrated attention on the actual workings of society Smith notes (as the radical democrats don't) that historical inequality caused by the division of labour is nevertheless *beneficial* to individuals whatever their special function in the system might be, from pin-making to the filling of ledgers. Inequality is not itself 'natural' but it is the result of natural *development*, the highly desirable general outcome of individuals' acting on their 'natural liberty', on the basis of formal equality which allows – indeed encourages – substantive inequality, substantive diversification.

Now wealth produced in society represents 'value', i.e. goods which are needed and desired by members of society and for which they are willing (as well as being compelled, though not necessarily in a harsh manner) to forego other goods. Value for Smith is of two kinds: use in direct consumption and the indirect utility of a good in exchange, on the market. Exchange-value, according to Smith, is not closely related to use-value, e.g. water has a very high value in use but not in exchange, and diamonds the other way round. What then determines the value of goods in exchange? Smith's conclusion is that it is *labour*:

> Labour was the first price, the original purchase money
> that was paid for all things. It was not by gold or by
> silver, but by labour, that all the wealth of the world was
> originally purchased and its value, to those who possess
> it, and who want to exchange it for some new productions,
> is precisely equal to the quantity of labour which it can
> enable them to purchase or command.

Smith presents this original 'labour theory of value' (such a crucial pillar of Marx's science of capital) as a kind of unveiling of a process which is not obvious to the eye, something that goes on underneath surface appearances, nothing but a general principle – it is this principle which Marx will in due course develop into his own concept of 'abstract labour'. Again, for Smith 'labour' refers to *labour commanded*, and not labour embodied, i.e. not just bare physical exertion in dealing with nature but including its social *context*. The later socialist development of this classical liberal theory of value (to be surveyed in the next lecture) could as a matter of fact be characterized as successive analyses and demolitions of the social context of labour, going with an increasingly narrower, more precise definition of labour itself *as* (nothing much more than) physical exertion. With this goes the shift from regarding 'value' only 'scientifically' to viewing it morally, as *desert*.

Smith's account of the distribution of wealth in civilized society is indeed 'cool' in the highest degree, that is to say, factual and dispassionate. He simply notes the fact that the value of products does not go to labour in its entirety. Labour receives 'wages' but there are also two other sources of revenue in society, viz. rent and profit. It just so happened in history that land came to be owned privately (yielding rent) and 'stock' was accumulated by 'undertakers' who employ labour and who receive profit on the active use of this stock, i.e. on their capital. Rent and profit are deductions from wage, not another kind of wage (as they are for later 'bourgeois apologists'). The distribution of revenue is unequal but not – in principle – unjust. The wages of labour are low, determined by the 'value' of labour in the market, but still labourers are much better off than they would be in the 'rude' state. In civilized society, with artificial restrictions on the productive employment of 'stock' being progressively lifted, the members of the 'three great, original and constituent orders of every civilized society' (i.e. landowners, entrepreneurs and labourers) receive in revenue what they *more or less* deserve, and thus the common good is promoted. In general the interests of the three orders dovetail and coincide, that is, in conditions of *expansion* which Smith envisaged for the future and of course intensely desired himself. The conclusion of *The Wealth of Nations*, in spite of Smith's cool manner in noting faults and making critical remarks about the prevailing system, is hence confident and impeccably liberal: it reasserts 'natural liberty' as the guarantee of just social relations and continuing prosperity.

However, we must note at least two important aspects of Smith's critique of civilized society, too. These may be subdued and intermittent in the text but they are of far-reaching importance for the future development of political economy, and in particular Marxism. *The Wealth of Nations* displays what might be best described as a kind of *fertile ambiguity* in respect of the position of 'undertakers' as well as labourers in civilized society. The interest of undertakers, as Smith recognizes, lies not just in expansion but also in the restriction of competition in the market. The rate of profit is high in poor and primitive economic conditions, and relatively low in fully developed ones. Undertakers thus will 'combine' in order to curtail the operations of the free market, in 'conspiracies against the public' which, as Smith wryly remarks, they are legally entitled to do, whereas labourers have not the liberty thus to combine. He has some pretty harsh words for 'dealers' who 'come from an order of men whose interest is never exactly the same with that of the public, who have generally an interest to deceive and even to oppress the public, and who accordingly have upon many occasions, both deceived and oppressed it'. And as regards labourers, while Smith certainly does not treat them with excessive sympathy and kindness – they are in general dull and meek, whereas undertakers are clever, bold, enterprising – he is not blind to their actual situation in 'civilized society'. He demands that labour should be properly 'valued' and labourers treated in accordance with 'equity'. Moreover he notes that the division of labour, while beneficial in general and historical terms, has also had lamentable short-term and particular effects on labourers who have had to undergo a process of 'mental mutilation'. This again – just to note in anticipation – reappears with vivid emphasis in Marx's strictures in the *Manuscripts* concerning the induced 'cretinism' of workers in capitalism. Smith's deadpan, cool political economy, that is to say, laying bare the 'criticism of the facts' themselves, joins Rousseau's heated and impassioned denunciation of the 'inauthenticity' of civilized life and society in being another important source of Marx's theory of alienation.

I hope that enough concrete detail has now been adduced from *The Wealth of Nations* to give us at least some *flavour* of the social idea of liberalism. I shall continue, in the next lecture, with the story of political economy after Smith, making some remarks on Ricardo and radical thinkers in Britain taking their cue from him. But before I turn to the next – and in many ways most difficult – topic under the present heading, the gestation of Marxism, one or two general observations on liberal political economy and its relationship to Marxism may be in order. The main point to grasp, it seems to me, is that the social idea of liberalism enters into Marx's thought – indeed we might say in a very substantial part *constitutes* Marx's thought – directly and positively, as distinguished from a mere 'critical' relationship existing between the two. The latter kind of relationship of course is very conspicuous, there to be seen: Marx *attacks* liberal political economy in no uncertain terms, he *denounces* the class system, he *castigates* profit as exploitation, envisages and wishes for the complete *abolition* of the division of labour, etc. But we have to endeavour to go deeper than the Marxist critique, noting here also what Marx accepts and assumes in his very criticism. Already some allusion has been made to this earlier but now, having sampled Adam Smith's doctrine, we can put the point in more precise terms. The following considerations would appear to me to be of particular importance.

Firstly, Marxism, too, is deliberately and self-consciously 'cool', occupying itself with the real world. In Marx's understanding of 'scientific socialism' quite clearly the emphasis is on 'scientific'; this is the quality of the doctrine which supposedly renders it superior to other versions of socialism; and the basic model for Marxist science is undoubtedly liberal political economy. Secondly, very much in the manner of Adam Smith, Marx too regards 'society' as the *real world*, the arena of economic transactions, livelihood concerns, material production and its organization. It is to this real world of society that in Marxism we see contraposed the fanciful, secondary worlds of politics, religion, culture, philosophy; 'science' befits primarily the former, not the latter. Thirdly, in the very critique that Marx advances against capitalism the 'criticism of the facts' plays a predominant role. Marx's main scientific achievement, in his own eyes, was the identification, description and analysis of the extraction of surplus value from labour in the process of capitalist production; but this Marxist theory of surplus value – of exploitation of man by man – is really not much more than the direct logical development of Smith's theory of value: the theory, if you like, of the social consequences of the exploitation of nature by human labour. Fourthly, Marxism accepts and indeed loudly proclaims the historical necessity of capitalism, the system of 'free enterprise' production which prepares the ground for socialism. That is to say, Marx does not as such deny the liberals' (i.e. Smith's) analysis of society or their moral values for that matter; he simply claims that history is now passing beyond the capitalist stage. Fifthly, Marx's scientific perspective rooted in liberal political economy remains very much to the fore even when he talks about the coming mighty proletarian revolution, the expected and desired 'turning of the world upside down' – there is nothing, of course, about *that* in Adam Smith. But Marx (as we briefly mentioned in the previous lecture) squarely predicates the revolution on the ripening of objective social forces, on secular developments in the techniques and organization of wealth-creation; his science, in other words, accompanies him also into the world of transcendence. And sixth and last, it can be argued that at least *in part* Marx's transcendent vision of communism is meant to be the realization of liberal values and ideals, a world of *enhanced* wealth-creation, a perfectly functioning society of producing, enterprising, self-regarding, amply consuming individuals who can now enjoy their 'natural liberty' to the full.

*   *   *

We turn now to the last big chapter in the story of the gestation of Marxism, the strand which I have entitled here the 'philosophical' idea of liberalism. The reference, of course, is concretely to the philosophy of G. W. F. Hegel whom Marx and Engels themselves looked upon as the highest, ultimate expression and representative of 'bourgeois' thought. But immediately we have to note an underlying – and most intriguing – paradox in the relationship of Marxism to Hegel. In a very real sense – in the sense of actual, palpable, substantive doctrinal chunks, in the *extensive* sense of visible, measurable 'inputs' – Hegelian philosophy adds very little, and nothing very important, to Marxism. On the one hand, it is to be noted that while Marx continued to pay the highest accolades to Hegel he also claimed to have totally discarded, destroyed, superseded Hegelian thought, stepping out of (and indeed annihilating) the world of 'philosophy' altogether. And on the other hand, there would be no difficulty at all in arguing that the modern background to Marxism (the elements present in its gestation period) is totally *exhausted* by reference to the two big departures in liberalism discussed in the foregoing. Marxism, that is to say, could be wholly accounted for in terms of the adaptation and synthesis of Rousseauist political theory and Smithian social science – as, of course, further developed in radical democracy and revolutionary communism in the one case, and labour economics and utopian socialism in the other (which themselves properly belong to the story of the 'formation', as distinguished from the 'gestation', of Marx's thought). Marx is a revolutionary social scientist, nothing more. There is no further room here for any addition or for 'philosophy' in this extensive sense. Hegel and Hegelianism are therefore in this perspective entirely otiose.

So why should one bother about Hegel? Here I would like to introduce a concept which it may initially be rather difficult to grasp but which is absolutely vital for a proper understanding of the genesis of Marxism. This concept is that of an *intensive* influence and relationship, or a vital connection in terms of a pervading spirit rather than palpable chunks of doctrine. What Marx inherits – assumes, adapts, transliterates, develops in a particular direction – is, I would like to argue, the spirit and historical momentum of the whole Hegelian enterprise; *this* is what is important for Marx, what makes Marxism itself important and distinctive as a social doctrine carrying on the mainstream European tradition, and not so much the actual expressions and categories taken over directly from Hegel (though the interest of these is by no means to be belittled). I shall therefore endeavour, to the best of my ability and within the space at my disposal, to offer at least a 'flavour' of the Hegelian enterprise, similarly to the way I have introduced Smith's political economy. To begin with, however, we have to acknowledge and appreciate this general point, as it were, negatively. Marx, whether one likes him or not, stands quite a few leagues higher than his immediate predecessors: revolutionary communists or socialist economists or utopian blueprinters. His doctrine is not the sum of communism and social science but rather their *product*. There is an extra *something* in Marx, not an 'ingredient' but rather a 'fermenting agent'; or, to vary the metaphor once again, there is a 'cement' of peculiar quality, with which a proper building is erected from the bricks of revolutionary transcendence and the cool knowledge of the workings of society. The 'synthesis' of these two modern departures is not an *easy* matter, it is not an obvious, comfortable way forward (except in historical retrospect!). On its own, revolutionary communism remains lingering in a heady but remote limbo of sublime principles and outlandish expectations. On its own, socialist political economy cannot free itself from the shackles of 'actual existence' which it may look at coolly but which it can attack only from a moralistic standpoint. Marx does follow the direction set by political economy and radical democracy but he places these two in a different *dimension*. It is this dimension, this fermentation, this 'lift', which accrues to Marxism from the spirit of the Hegelian enterprise. Thus, on a closer look we might indeed be tempted to turn the paradox on its head and say that Hegel – the highest expression of the 'philosophical' idea of liberalism – provides *everything* that is important and interesting in Marxism.

What, then, is Hegel on about? Let us say frankly: nobody is quite sure, including the most learned of commentators or for that matter the philosopher's students, contemporaries, immediate successors who directly after the death of their master proceeded to group themselves into an Hegelian 'Right' and an Hegelian 'Left' (with a 'Centre', too, of course), all claiming orthodoxy. In retrospect it seems – and I hope that this does not sound too much of a sleight-of-hand – that they were all of them correct, presenting their case validly or at least plausibly. Hegel's philosophy is *essentially* 'ambiguous' – in the true sense of the word – pointing in several directions, amenable to various and contrary interpretations; which is of course *not at all* to say that it is meaningless, self-contradictory or inconsequential. On the very contrary, Hegel's is the most profound and most dramatic influence on modern European thought, in areas of culture far away from and beyond Marxism, more and more recognized for its interest and value by the cognoscenti. We cannot of course even begin to appreciate Hegel's stature here – not four but forty lectures would scarcely be adequate to the task. I shall try merely to indicate Hegel's significance as a philosopher of mainstream liberalism in and for the gestation of Marxism; and I shall adopt an interpretation of Hegel which – whatever else it might be – seems to make sense in the context of the genesis of Marxism. This interpretation will also show Marx's own understanding of Hegel to be – if not necessarily a hundred per cent valid – at least a sensible one.

Three ideas in Hegel will need to be highlighted here. The first is Hegel's concept of 'spirit'. The second is his 'dialectic'. And the third is his philosophical theory of the modern state and society. Starting with 'spirit', it will be recalled that earlier in this lecture I referred a couple of times to the 'soaring thought' of liberalism, naming this as the third partner in a trinity of values, together making up the liberal paradigm; the other two are equality and free enterprise. My use of the expression, 'soaring thought', is not at all frivolous; it has a pointed reference to the Hegelian enterprise. It is Hegel's idea of 'spirit' which best epitomizes this soaring, climbing, restless, transcendent quality of human thought, human activity and human history. The idea of spirit in Hegel, as far as it can be ascertained, has a number of historical sources and just as many significations and connotations. Its derivation is highly complex and can be traced back to classical Greek idealism, Christianity, Kantian philosophy and Germanic folklore. In various textual locations in Hegel spirit has primary reference to God, to the Holy Spirit, to the community or the nation, to thinking, knowledge, philosophy, creative human action, and quite a lot of other things. The later Marxist equation of the Hegelian spirit with human 'labour', though somewhat restricted, does not seem to be unorthodox or out of place either. The main point about spirit though in Hegel is that for him it is *that which is active* in reality; spirit is the prime mover, actor and knower, the first principle and element of vitality in everything in experience, the 'substance' which is also 'subject'. Spirit is ultimate reality, the whole of reality, and the last word in reality, the Alpha and Omega and all the letters of the Greek alphabet in between. Spirit is the world and at the same time it is the *transcendence* of the world. Furthermore – and this is a specific and emphatic aspect of Hegel's philosophy – the very essence of spirit is pronounced to be *self-differentiation*. To put it in a nutshell; in the Hegelian scheme spirit creates the world or 'nature' (what we would loosely call 'empirical reality') in the first place. Hence spirit is embodied in nature. However, nature at the same time is to be seen as the 'other' of spirit, its negation. Nature provides resistance and opposition; the life and essence of spirit therefore consist in *overcoming* this opposition.

Hegel was nineteen years of age only when the French Revolution broke out and this event, 'the bursting forth of freedom', apparently exerted a decisive influence on him. Spirit, as he saw it, was now fully visible and triumphant in the human world, too. Here the definition of spirit as *freedom* comes to the fore; spirit is freedom and freedom is spirit. History is defined as the growth in the consciousness of freedom and in Hegel's understanding it is the revolutionary era which now proclaims and loudly demonstrates that human beings as such, as *bearers of spirit*, are in essence free, every single one of them. Although in the narrower political sense Hegel never was what we might call a 'revolutionary' or 'radical' – his stance was that of mainstream liberalism, turning later into conservatism – the message of his philosophy as a whole, declaring spirit thus to be superior to actual existence, and defining human nature in terms of freedom, yet was and remained revolutionary in this most profound sense. The human spirit – epitomizing the overriding power of reason and the essential *freedom of reason* – was marching on, conquering and transforming 'objective' reality, and 'recognizing' itself more and more clearly in the world outside. It is I think somewhat misleading, if not crudely procrustean, to draw a sharp distinction between Hegel's 'method' (i.e. revolutionary) and his 'system' (i.e. conservative), as his radical disciples, including Marx, were to do later. Undoubtedly, however, there is a permanent and exciting *tension* between this overall revolutionary message and particular aspects of Hegel's philosophy, a disturbing discrepancy, if you like, between the deep current and the ripples appearing on the surface. In its deeper significance, spirit in Hegel does give expression to the pure spirit of modernity, of modern humanism, the 'soaring thought' of progressive liberalism, now being confronted with the outcome of its own historical achievements.

Hegel's most outstanding work, *The Phenomenology of Spirit* (1807) – one of the most ambitious, fantastic and influential

philosophical treatises ever written – clearly displays this fundamental tension. Of its vast and extremely complicated content,
I shall pick out three points only, those with a more direct
relevance to our overall concerns here. Firstly, Hegel accounts
for the historical triumph of the principle of human equality in
dramatic terms, involving a struggle between the 'master' and
the 'bondsman' which results in the complete victory of the
latter and the complete 'annihilation' of the former. The point
about this – in view of Marx's stance later on – is that the
superiority of the bondsman over the master in Hegel's terms
consists very clearly in his *direct* contact with nature through
labouring. The second point to note is that while Hegel emphatically endorses the principle of revolution (i.e. the French Revolution), he notes in this treatise the danger of 'absolute freedom'
turning into 'absolute terror'. The revolution, if carried too far
in one direction, consumes and destroys itself; extreme individualism begets extreme authoritarianism; the storming of the
Bastille *could* lead to the reign of the guillotine. In this seemingly
'conservative' onslaught on radical democracy (i.e. on Rousseau's spiritual heirs) there is also the message – well heeded by
Marx – that proper progress by mankind must involve the
consolidation of social relations and even more importantly the
willing acceptance of the continuing role played by 'objective'
factors, i.e. nature, in human affairs. A distant but audible echo
of this Hegelian counsel of caution is heard much later in Marx's
memorable words concerning 'everlasting natural necessity' in
the third volume of *Capital*. Thirdly, Hegel's grand conclusion
in the *Phenomenology* is the category of 'absolute knowledge',
the highest level of self-consciousness attained by the spirit;
this signifies, however, continuing activity and struggle, spirit's
adventures being in the proper sense *free* and thus *unpredictable*.
Again, in the Marxist adaptation this is paralleled by Marx's
staunch refusal (in this being almost alone among modern
radical thinkers) to define exactly, or predict in concrete terms,
the nature of future communist society. Mankind in communism
is *spirit* and therefore *free*; communism therefore cannot be fully
comprehended from our present vantage-point.

I turn now to the famous Hegelian 'dialectic'. There is, strictly
speaking, no 'dialectical method' in Hegel – in the sense of a

particular reasoning technique, to be employed or discarded at will – and neither is there a clear, well-defined 'doctrine' of dialectic as a distinct part of the Hegelian philosophical system (except for one chapter in Hegel's *Encyclopaedia*). We find, of course, a great many incisive but scattered references to dialectic in the texts but these do not make up a separate, identifiable and substantial body of teaching. Yet – and this, in a way, curiously parallels the nature of the Hegelian influence on Marx (*intensive*, rather than extensive) – dialectic, or the dialectical approach, *infuses* the whole of Hegel's philosophy. Everything in Hegel is 'dialectical'. So what are we talking about? We are talking about a very ancient, very deeply imbedded (and very exciting) tradition of Western thought the essential characteristic of which is the understanding of reality in terms of *movement*. (Here we might recall briefly the somewhat stark comments made in the previous lecture about certain distinguishing features of the European tradition; these highlight the concepts of reason, struggle, movement, freedom – all of them related to dialectic!) It seems to me that as far as Hegel is concerned (who acknowledges the ancient as well as the modern sources of his view) the best way to understand dialectic is through the concept of 'spirit', already encountered above in our meagre effort to make sense of Hegelian philosophy. Dialectic, quite simply, is the description of the life and nature of spirit. It sets out, *generalizes* the essential activity of spirit in creating its opposite, nature, and then successively overcoming this opposition and finally recognizing itself, its own work, in the opposition thus overcome. Since spirit is everything and is everywhere, this basic *pattern of movement* is – so Hegel seems to argue – to be found in all of reality, and in all branches of intellectual inquiry. Just grasp this: the world around us and within us, nature, history, culture, religion, and everything else conceivable, is nothing but a gigantic *argument* conducted by spirit with *itself*, with its own created and mutually opposed forms of appearance. Weird, maybe, but not without its strange fascination and tremendous momentum to which the subsequent history of Western philosophy – including the doctrine of Marxism – is eloquent testimonial.

There is nothing rigid, cut-and-dried, 'scientific' or even

'logical' (in the textbook sense of logic) in the Hegelian dialectic: it is philosophy on the threshold of myth, religious poetry, abstract literary fiction. No 'three laws of dialectic', as in Engels and Stalin – it is noteworthy, in this context, that Marx himself never attempted to flesh out any dialectical laws; he himself was very close to the 'spirit' of the Hegelian enterprise, as we shall see later. Dialectic is suggestive and 'speculative' – to use one of Hegel's favourite terms; its more precise working, unfolding, always depends on the subject matter at hand. But if we wanted to reduce its rich complexity to some sort of a schematic order – for didactic purposes, as it were – we could say something like this. Dialectic in Hegel involves *three assertions* about reality: that reality is interdependent, that it is progressive, and that it is ultimately 'spiritual' or ideal. Reality is interdependent: we have observed this already, in the brief account given of Hegel's concept of spirit. Spirit *must* create its opposite, nature, this is its very life, its mode of existence. God without the universe is an empty abstraction, the universe without God is unintelligible. Everything is complex, the unity of opposites, and it is the opposition – more dramatically: 'self-contradiction' – that gives *meaning* to the objects of our thought and makes thinking possible in the first place. Hegel invites us to think, in a celebrated section of his *Science of Logic*, of the simplest, barest notion possible, viz. 'being' – but the point is that we cannot; in the process of *thinking* it 'being' turns into its very opposite, 'nothing'.

Which leads to the second assertion: reality is progressive. In thinking, and indeed in everything, we are being inevitably led forward: spirit marches on. Movement is progression, and not just that, it is *progress*, moving towards the better, the fuller, the more adequate understanding, the more satisfactory perspective. Reality is argument, not a slanging match. There is always a first assertion, an act of creation if you like, a 'position'; this position is countered, opposed; then the two are united, reconciled in a higher position. This 'three-beat rhythm' (as a Hegel-scholar once aptly called it) of reality goes on relentlessly. Triadicity, though not applied uniformly or mechanically, is present in all the Hegelian texts, denoted by a number of terms, which can sometimes be quite confusing. For example, Hegel talks about spirit 'in-itself', spirit 'for-itself' (i.e. distant from, opposing itself), and spirit 'in-and-for itself'; and about the 'abstract universal' opposed by the 'particular', and the opposition overcome by the 'concrete universal'. The third, crowning 'moment' of dialectic has special significance. Hegel calls it *Aufhebung*, deliberately, since this term in German has a *double* meaning; it means both cancellation and preservation. In English even a neologism was coined in acknowledgement of this significance, viz 'sublation'; another expressive translation of *Aufhebung* is 'suspension' (i.e. 'holding up' *and/or* 'ceasing'), as used for instance in the Introduction to Martin Nicolaus' translation of Marx's *Grundrisse*. *Aufhebung* or 'negation of negation' (another pregnant Hegelian term, beloved of Marxists) is not a return to the first position but a *new* position which itself leads to a new negation, and so on and so on. In history a relevant example for the Hegelian 'negation of negation' is the *restoration state* in Europe, or constitutional monarchy, which 'reconciles' the ancient tradition of monarchy and the net result of revolution (after the excesses of 'absolute freedom' and 'absolute terror' are eliminated), establishing the modern principle of constitutionalism.

The third assertion involved in the Hegelian dialectic is that reality is 'ideal' or 'spiritual'. This is the point where, it should be noted here briefly, Hegel and some of his 'leftwing' followers, including Marx, will be seen to part company. The leftwing or radical development of Hegelian philosophy can, I think, be correctly described as so many, successive and cumulative, attempts to *redefine* Hegel's concept of 'spirit' in non-idealistic terms, i.e. as human self-consciousness, sensuous human nature, or labouring activity (as in Marx's case). Now it is pretty obvious that from this radical point of view Hegel's 'idealism' – his insistence on defining spirit *as* spirit, as supra-personal and supra-sensuous reality – will appear anathema, to be attacked and dismissed. Whether it is reasonable or valid to discard Hegelian idealism and *at the same time* to hold on to a 'dialectical perspective' is a rather moot question which I do not propose to tackle here. In subsequent lectures there will be an opportunity to comment further on this problem – obviously very central to a proper understanding of Marxism. For now, at any rate, let us note that for Hegel the dialectical progression of reality does mean the demonstration of its ideal character. Reality becomes fully and finally 'real', as it were, in the thinking mind, in reason, thought, philosophy. Rational thought – 'thought thinking itself' – is superior to everything else, it is the culmination of all experience, the very proof of the existence of the universe. Philosophy, pure thought, stands at the pinnacle of the vast Hegelian system, as 'absolute spirit' which has super-seded, and incorporated in itself, the experiences of natural existence, history, creative art and revealed religion. The last word is the philosopher's who 'comprehends his time in thought,' who *alone* fully understands that 'what is rational is real, and what is real is rational'. For Hegel therefore history *ends* in philosophy ('ends' not in a temporal but in a logical sense), and thus *qua* idealist philosopher Hegel has no interest whatever in the future – a conclusion which baffled and irritated his leftwing followers.

The two famous quotes above are taken from the Preface to Hegel's *Philosophy of Right*, his main substantive text in the field of social and political theory. It is to this text that we shall have to turn now, in order to introduce the *third* important idea of Hegel's in the context of the gestation of Marxism. Readers will surely find this more congenial than the foregoing rather terse account of Hegel's spirit and dialectic; the latter, however, in view of Marx's deep-structural relationship to Hegel, could not be avoided. With this third idea we are resuming the story of classical European liberalism, which we left off with liberal 'society' (Smith's individuals pursuing their natural liberty) occupying the centre of the stage. The fundamental problem of the social idea of liberalism, as we have already hinted, is that it cannot as such reconcile its own principal starting premise of human equality (equal natural rights) and the substantive inequality following on the liberation of (*formally* equal) indi-vidual enterprise. Formal equality, as it were, runs amuck: short of the very drastic and transcendent remedy of radical or 'totalitarian' democracy (issuing in revolutionary communism), disturbingly but in a way *quite naturally* it generates a society very different from what was foreseen or (in the case of some early liberal thinkers at any rate) consciously intended. In the life of modern society the principle of equality is pushed to the background, rendered innocuous, and therewith goes the collective moral identity of the people. On the one hand the morality of individual self-regard, or rather self-aggrand-izement, fills out the content of freedom, rights and equality, and on the other hand the pursuit of wealth-creation as the human aim and activity *par excellence* more and more enhances divisions of wealth and thereby the conflict of classes. Liberal society is 'atomistic' society and by the same token 'class' society. Now it could be argued that the essence of Hegelian political thought, as it appears in retrospect, is an endeavour to bestow *unity*, and a concrete moral identity, on liberal society while at the same time preserving it as a 'society', i.e. with continuing free individual enterprise. It is questionable whether or not the endeavour is successful – it certainly isn't, in Marxist terms, and to be sure Marx's rejection of *this* aspect of Hegelianism is almost one hundred per cent.

Hegel's *Philosophy of Right*, it must be said, is rather a drab text, with only faint residues of the 'soaring thought' characterizing the *Phenomenology*. But it does have its own cleverness, intellectual force and aesthetic appeal, and besides this text shows up very poignantly the fundamental problems and essential ambiguity of liberal political philosophy. 'Dialec-tic', in the sense described above, has only a shadowy appearance here; instead Hegel presents us with static and rigid categories, of the various interlocking layers of modern life and social structure; nevertheless, 'triadicity' is still present. *The Phil-osophy of Right* depicts 'spirit objective' in the modern world, i.e. (in commonsensical interpretation) the imposition of human will, human reason, on the world of nature, and the concomitant creation of a fully 'rational' social and political structure. Note that, broadly speaking, this 'conquest' of the world by spirit proceeds in three directions: towards inanimate nature, towards society, and towards the self. The very *structure* of Hegel's 'objective spirit' is of course not just reminiscent, but indeed it is the immediate parent, of the structure of what we designated Marx's three-pronged doctrine of 'human liberation' in the previous lecture. Spirit as 'will' asserts itself against nature, conquers it, possesses it, uses it; this is what Hegel calls 'right' in the abstract. 'Right' signifies, further, contractual relations among individuals in respect of their ownership of nature, which in turn brings in the institution of punishment. Now spirit as it were turns inward and produces the realm of 'morality', with its notions and sentiments of 'duty' and 'conscience'. But this second level in the world of objective spirit is also pronounced by Hegel 'abstract', in that it contains no concrete reference to what duties actually *are*, which moral feelings are valid and which are not. Here then we enter, as the moment of dialectical reconciliation, the realm of *concrete ethics* (as one learned translation renders the German *Sittlichkeit*), i.e. the 'society' of concrete peoples, historical nations, with their ethos and cultural tradition, their laws, governments, social relations.

The dialectic of *Sittlichkeit* presents us again with three moments. Firstly, human beings are united in the 'family' in a purely 'natural' manner, based on sexual attraction, personal love, intimacy, the need to beget and rear children. But the identity of the family is not fully 'rational' in Hegel's terms, as it restricts the growth of individual personality, is inward-looking, and by its nature ephemeral: when children grow up, the family (logically speaking) ceases to function. Here then we encounter the realm of human existence which for Hegel appears as the *negation* of unity, a realm where morality is merely 'inversely reflected'. This is called 'civil' or 'bourgeois society', the arena of individuals acting individually: producing, exchanging, consuming – in fact, this is Adam Smith's 'natural society', containing certain advantages over the family but not without its own warts and blemishes. Civil society liberates and enhances 'particularity' or diversity in human affairs and relations; it produces wealth and ever more sophisticated appetites to consume it; its intricate division of labour provides personal fulfilment in work but also – as Hegel recognizes clearly – class distinctions. While the general principle, as it were, of civil society is fully rational and justified, its actual *working* in modern times induces Hegel to make some rather hard-sounding critical remarks which some interpreters have seen as traces of 'antediluvian' Marxism even. To be sure, the resemblance to the tone, terms and logical sweep of the later Marxist 'critique of political economy' is uncanny. See, for example, this oft-quoted 'prophetic' passage:

> When Civil Society is in a state of unimpeded activity, it
> is engaged in expanding internally in population and
> industry. The amassing of wealth is intensified by
> generalizing (a) the linkage of men by their needs, and
> (b) the methods of preparing and distributing the means
> to satisfy these needs, because it is from this double
> process of generalization that the largest profits are
> derived. That is one side of the picture. The other side is
> the sub-division and restriction of particular jobs. This
> results in the dependence and distress of the class tied to
> work of that sort, and these again entail inability to feel
> and enjoy the broader freedoms and especially the
> intellectual benefits of Civil Society.

But, for better or worse, Hegel's 'social criticism' in the *Philosophy of Right* is not followed through in a manner which would please radicals. Instead, the dialectic jumps once more and from civil society we move on to what is the climactic point of Hegel's political thought, the category of *state* which Hegel (reputedly) called in his lectures in Berlin the 'march of God on earth'. But even the printed eulogies of the state in *The Philosophy of Right* would, to be sure, sound very jarring and fulsome to Anglo-Saxon 'liberal' ears especially, so perhaps we should at this point give the reassurance that, although his language and framework are rather different, Hegel is still basically talking here about the *liberal* state, i.e. the constitutional and limited state, the state which is legally sovereign and morally autonomous but which still, not only *allows* the free functioning of civil society, with its private enterprise and class system, but is in fact called upon to protect and preserve the same by superimposing on it a higher kind of *unity*, a new, 'rational' identity and collective morality. Viewed from the perspective of developing liberalism, the point here is surely that – unlike Smith – Hegel refuses to accept 'civil society' as being alone 'substantial' or 'natural' but notes that it *requires* the profounder substantiality of the state; and further that unlike Rousseau's collective 'general will' Hegel's state incorporates internal differentiation and thus effectively salvages the modern principle of free enterprise. Freedom and equality, Rousseau and Smith, the political and social ideas of liberalism are thus – in point of *theory* at any rate – 'reconciled' in what Marx clearly regarded as the highest *philosophical* expression of the modern 'bourgeois epoch'.

To conclude then, briefly, on this rather difficult topic. Concerning the significance of Hegelian philosophy in the gestation of Marxism, three points, it seems to me, are deserving of special emphasis – in concordance with the three ideas in Hegel I endeavoured to highlight in the foregoing. Hegel enters into Marxism, that is to say, on three levels simultaneously. It is Hegel's mighty, all-conquering 'spirit' which, interpreted as *human labour*, provides Marx with his basic principle of transcendence, the uncompromising radicalism, revolutionary thrust and confidence of his doctrine: humanity, reason, the freedom of reason, will conquer. No more needs to be said about this right now; the transformation (or development, if you like) of Hegel's spirit at the hand of Marx's Left Hegelian teachers will be commented on in the next lecture. Hegel's generalized 'dialectical' perspective, in the second place, serves as a kind of primitive structural model (though probably not much more than that) for Marx's theory of social conflict and the succession of historical stages, and also a part of the *logical language* of Marx's critical science of capital. Marx definitely assumes social and historical reality to be 'interdependent' as well as 'progressive'. But I do not intend hereafter to make too much heavy weather of the Hegelian dialectical heritage for Marxism, mainly for two reasons. On the one hand, the story of the genesis of Marxism, as understood in these pages, stops with the formulation of Marx's own individual standpoint, i.e. the concept of 'alienated labour', in the *Manuscripts* of 1844, and this predates both the Marxist theory of history and the Marxist science of political economy. And on the other hand, I suspect, the 'dialectical' character of Marx's social science is these days in danger of being somewhat exaggerated by enthusiastic commentators; on this point I myself would find greater sympathy with Marx's and Engels' *own* judgment of the matter, viz. that

Marxist political economy is in principle proper 'science', that is, factual and observational, capable of empirical corroboration or refutation, and hence in no need of any philosophical underpinning.

We need to say just a bit more, however, concerning the third point of entry of Hegelianism into Marxism. This is in fact quite a fascinating topic on its own. I have said above that Hegel's category of 'state' is the *liberal* state, in its essential function and features. Now this is not strictly speaking true or rather it is not 'the whole truth'. Hegel's state is the liberal state, unquestionably, as it is meant to be the completion and great reconciler of the conflictual relationships of liberal 'civil society'. But at the same time this Hegelian state *spills over* simultaneously in two opposed directions. We can make here the following rough-and-ready distinction, in order to explain this. On one hand, the concrete elements of Hegel's state are decidedly *conservative*, if not archaic, in comparison with a great deal of mainstream 'liberal' thinking of Hegel's own times, e.g. Hegel has no truck with universal suffrage or even territorial representation as such, he wants to preserve an hereditary estate in the legislature, his 'constitutional monarch' is more than a figurehead, etc. Marx, indeed, mercilessly exposes and destroys later what he calls the 'medievalism' of Hegel's political theory. However, at the same time one can detect an underlying abstract *principle* of the state in Hegel – a willowy, ghost-like presence – which definitely points forward precisely towards the kind of radical development carried out in Marx's own work. This principle is robustly egalitarian and holistic, conjuring up the spirit of the ancient Greek city, the 'majestas' of the early modern theory of sovereignty, and even the idea of radical democracy as adumbrated in Rousseau. This is the pure principle of state as 'moral community', expressing the absolutely superior will of human beings united in virtue and goodness, transcending their particular differences and conflicts in actual existence. Now take the concrete institutional details away and apply this pure principle of state directly *to* actual existence, making it devour 'society' instead of merely containing it, and you have the most pristine and exciting idea of *communism* in front of you. Marx's concept of communism contains of course a lot more besides this pure moral element, and the latter is considerably diluted, if not confounded, especially in the 'mature' Marxist texts. However, it could be cogently argued that it is precisely the Hegelian connection – communism as the philosophical 'absolute', as Hegel's principle of state further purified and transliterated – which elevates the Marxist understanding of the 'good society' above corresponding notions found with other departures in modern socialist thought.

*   *   *

The somewhat unsensational but nonetheless relevant conclusion with which we have to end this lecture is that mainstream European liberalism – bourgeois thought in its progressive phase – leaves a number of fundamental theoretical and practical problems unresolved. The principle of equality, as we have seen, itself raises the issue of natural liberty which in turn conjures up the problem of class conflict. The Hegelian state, with which we have concluded the expository part of the lecture, is a splendid *tour de force* in an attempt to reconcile these two basic principles of liberalism (freedom and equality) but this conception of the state is itself volatile, unstable; at its worst it provides merely an 'academic' solution, at its best it shows its chief value by being a 'fertile' influence in further development, from liberalism to socialism.

In the light of this interpretation of the concealed 'gestation' of Marxist thought, it might then be surmised that Marxism takes off, as it were, *directly* from Hegel, since Hegelianism *ex hypothesi* represents the highest and most philosophical expression of liberalism. But this is not as simple as that. We might as well note right here two curious aspects of Marx's development. In the first place it is a mere historical and biographical fluke, if you like, that Marx's development *begins* with Hegelianism, proceeds on to the absorption of revolutionary communism, and then culminates in the adoption and perfection of the stance of the science of political economy. But this direction of Marx's own intellectual progression would not really be intelligible – except as a secular, and in itself insignificant, sequence of events – if Hegelianism really, exhaustively, embodied *all* that was dynamic, progressive, fertile, influential in mainstream liberal thought. Why should then Marx 'return' to revolutionary communists, the heirs of Rousseau, and settle with political economy, the tradition built up by Adam Smith and his liberal followers? The only sensible answer, it seems to me, is that the Hegelian 'philosophical' apex of the liberal perspective is not, in truth, an exhaustive summary of all that which acquires importance for the development of Marxism. *For* liberal society it may well be that the Hegelian philosophical state is the last, and perfect, answer. *For* socialism, however, and for Marxist doctrine in particular, this is only *one* culmination among others, one 'peak' as it were in the company of other peaks. Socialism, therefore, takes off from all these 'peaks' together, at the same time, and in synthetic union; Marxism is *not* just the further development, perfection, 'disclosure' of Hegelianism; it is the further development, *equally*, of the political, social and philosophical ideas expressing the essential nature of liberal thought.

This consideration then will bring into even sharper focus the other – and very closely related – curious aspect involved in the gestation of Marxism, one which attentive readers will have probably noted already. It is that the historical and what I have called 'logical' progression of liberalism contains a reversive – indeed retrogressive – element. Its going forward is revealed at the same time as a going backward. The most 'primitive' expression of liberal thought – the doctrine of equal natural rights, popular sovereignty, radical democracy – is also its most *explosive expression*, the one with the greatest historical momentum, the departure which leads directly to revolutionary communism ('primitive' or not), i.e. it issues in the starkest denial of liberalism. The more sophisticated expression of liberalism as embodied in the 'social' idea – wealth-creation, natural liberty, free enterprise – is still no doubt politically progressive but already with a hitch, an historical arrest, a discrepancy which makes it incline more and more towards conservatism, settlement, consolidation. That is to say, its abstract principle is still political equality but its practice – and practical apologetics – becomes concentrated on the protection of social inequality. And finally while the philosophical idea of liberalism, as we have seen with Hegel, is the most explosive and revolutionary on the *narrow front* of transcendent, speculative ideas (spirit, dialectic, state) it is at the same time the most markedly conservative, if not reactionary, in its concrete political aspects. I don't know, frankly, whether or not there was any kind of historical 'necessity' in this double process of progression–retrogression and alas I haven't got the assurance of a dedicated Marxist to argue that the discrepancy noted here demonstrates the final bankruptcy of liberal thought (and 'bourgeois' society with it). It is not for us, it seems to me, as students of the genesis of Marxism as a chapter in the history of ideas, to say that liberalism *had* to decline and socialism in general and Marxism in particular *had* to follow on. Our interest here is in trying to find out – once we have accepted that socialism in general and Marxism in particular are, so to speak, 'on the table' – why they have their distinctive shape and colouring, and not some other. As regards Marx's thought, as it emerges from its phase of gestation into its formative period, the above described curious heterogeneity and 'reverse–progressing' character of liberalism will go, I hope, at least some way towards explaining the curious nature of the 'synthesis' said to be embodied in that thought.

Thus we take our leave of the world of liberalism. Marxism grows out of the political, social and philosophical ideas of liberalism synthetically, containing these three ideas in an approximately equal measure; they all have their significance for Marxist development. However, there is intervening – and indeed very substantial and pertinent – a period of *socialist* and *radical* articulation of these very same ideas, coming forth in a thoroughgoing critique of liberalism, which will bestow on Marxism its final and visible 'form'. It will be both historically accurate and at the same time advantageous for us to trace this socialist and radical formulation in sequence, in the interpretive terms adopted for this lecture. The political idea of liberalism, that is to say, will be traced next right up to its climax in the socialist pursuit of 'real equality'; the social idea to its issuing in the advocacy of the interests of 'labour' and the apotheosis of 'co-operation', with reference also to utopian socialism; and the philosophical idea to its final culmination in radical humanism. We shall then be in a position directly to gaze upon – take in, confront, contemplate – the actual *fruits* of this lengthy, complex but enthralling, development, i.e. the thought of Marx.

FORMATION

I feel obliged to begin this lecture by advancing, so to speak, a disjunctive judgment, the tedious and circumspect academic 'on the one hand' and 'on the other hand'. The early phase in the life of modern socialism (doctrine and movement) is obviously a very important chapter in the story of the genesis of Marxism. The visible 'form' of Marxist thought, as I said before, is largely – indeed, overwhelmingly – derived from ideas found in Marx's immediate radical predecessors and contemporaries; Marx shares their values, adopts and adapts their language and concepts. But, to be sure, this socialist and radical legacy pertains to the outward 'form' of Marxism only, or certainly not much more than to this form. The inner core or 'substance' of Marxism is just as much the development of the European *mainstream* as it is the offspring of modern political radicalism. Perhaps, in the spirit of the opening lines of the first lecture, we could go even further than this, suggesting that the mainstream – in this case progressive liberalism – is in fact more important for Marxism than its 'negation' in early socialism. As I endeavoured to argue in the previous lecture: in at least two dimensions out of three, namely concerning the *science* of society and the *philosophy* of communism and of historical change, Marxism takes its cue directly from the 'bourgeois' giants, from Smith, Ricardo and Hegel. Admittedly, in the dimension I have called the 'political idea' of liberalism, i.e. radical democracy, matters are not so clear. Here it could be argued the later development of revolutionary communism has a more direct, and substantive, significance for Marxism than its original phase, namely the Rousseauist notion of the 'sovereign people'. But again, paradoxically, it is this 'political' premise of Marxism which tends to be suppressed, smothered under the weight of Marx's philosophical (in the early texts) and scientific (in the mature writings) doctrines. The 'supersession' of politics *in* Marxist doctrine reflects its suppressed state *for* Marxist doctrine, which means also its relegation to a theoretical 'backseat' in the genesis of Marxism. And yet the revolutionary communist major premise, concealed or not, still remains one of Marx's 'absolute pre-suppositions'. But we'll come to this later, in the appropriate section of this lecture.

The point, then, is that on the one hand the significance of early communist, socialist and radical humanist departures can easily be over-emphasized. Marx, while adopting their values and language, *reacts* to them and *negates* them, just as forcefully as he reacts to and negates mainstream liberalism. The early socialists provide, in a way, the foil which forces Marx towards his grand synthesis of all the dimensions involved. However, on the other hand it would be a grave error to assume an air of supercilious arrogance *vis-à-vis* these doctrines and movements – as, I am afraid, Marx himself does quite frequently. I should like to recall here – and assert with added emphasis – a general point I made in the first lecture. The early socialists are not just to be seen as 'predecessors' of Marx, whose sole – or even main – significance for the student of the history of political thought is that Marxist teaching grew 'synthetically' out of them. Not only do they have an interest and value of their own; it could also be said that they are, in a way unfairly and unhelpfully, *belittled* by the limelight given to the Marxist synthesis. Impressive as it undoubtedly is – in the intellectual realm as well as in the arena of practical politics – the Marxist synthesis somehow embraces and achieves 'too much': in its grand sweep of unification and theoretical advancement it has, under a smooth, glossy surface, an element of inner tension and heterogeneity not present with the socialist forerunners. The latter are, perhaps, simplistic, primitive and too one-sided in contrast to Marxism; yet they have an exciting and appealing homogeneity about them, later lost in the whirlwind of history. They are – to adapt one of Marx's celebrated *obiter dicta* here – like the ancient Greeks in representing the purity, optimism and dynamic momentum of a civilization in its youth. In other words, the Marxist synthesis may not have been as completely, unreservedly and irreversibly a victory as one might be tempted to judge at first. At the end of this lecture I shall essay a few reflections to explain the point more fully.

But on with our story. We have, in a heuristic manner, identified in the previous lecture three central ideas in modern liberal thought, as this thought figures in the gestation of Marxism. It will be at least as useful, if not more so, to continue with this heuristic classification and present early socialist and radical thought, as figuring in the formation of Marxism, sequentially in the same terms. We shall, that is to say, argue that the political idea of liberalism issues in revolutionary communism, the social idea in utopian socialism (in a broad sense, as I shall explain later), and the philosophical idea in radical humanism. From this point on, however, we ought to render the vital connection between this emerging genealogical picture and what we earlier termed Marx's three-pronged doctrine of human liberation more explicit. This could not have been done very easily in our discussion of liberalism where the lines are still blurred – and this is one telling reason why liberalism could reasonably be characterized as the historical plane within which Marxism merely 'gestates'. But now the connection begins to surface. The 'political' idea is that which highlights human liberation from the point of view of society, the group, the collectivity, the species – liberation primarily in the relationship of human to human. The 'social' idea it is that focuses on the human relationship to nature, highlighting the world of labour, production, the organisation of production, and also the human consumption of nature, the enjoyments of the fruits of labour. And crowning it all, the 'philosophical' idea projects the liberation of the human mind, the independent and conquering human spirit, the transcendence and potency of reason. I need hardly emphasize that these three dimensions of human liberation – in the case of modern radicalism and socialism as well as with Marx – connote *predominant*, as distinguished from exclusive, concerns: political revolutionaries are not unaware of the problem of production and consumption, humanist philosophers are not indifferent to social organization, and 'utopians', so-called, do have a critical mind. And nor should we take the conventional cultural-national labels too literally: humanists, socialists and revolutionaries are found in France,

Germany and England in abundance, co-operating and cross-fertilizing. Here, too, it is relative predominance which counts. On the other hand I *would* emphasize – so as not to lose it from our interpretive gaze – that all three dimensions of human liberation do represent the 'modern synthesis' of the perspectives of transcendence and understanding in their peculiar ways; they all contain, quite explicitly and indeed aggressively, the assertion that fulfilment, perfection, the 'good society', is within reach of human reason and effort. It is this fusion of heaven and earth that Marx's thought ultimately inherits and expresses – together with its underlying problems.

It may be – at some little danger of procrustean simplification – advantageous now to further 'distil' the three major departures involved in the formation of Marxism. We need as sharp a focus as we can reasonably obtain. I suggest, therefore, that in the case of revolutionary communism what should be highlighted is the idea of *virtue*, of egalitarian purity and fervour, the will and desire to raise individuals to a higher moral level, absorbing them in the community. Nearest to the perspective of transcendence in the tradition, if you like, the moral puritanism of the revolutionary communist departure is well complemented by the 'coolness' – icy cold, to be sure – of its uncompromising militancy, its tendency to see things in sharp black-and-white contrast. In the case of utopian socialism and germane varieties, I think, the notion of *happiness* should be given special stress and elevation, or fulfilment in the sense of immediate palpable gratification by actual flesh-and-blood individuals (and mainly *of* their flesh and blood). Lying closest to the world of 'actual existence', the lukewarmness – and I mean this in an illustrative, not a denigratory, sense – of this more moderate, sedate departure in socialism in respect of *aims* is perfectly matched by its moderate, relative meekness regarding preferred *methods* of social change. The extreme, often fantastic, rhetoric associated with utopian socialism should not deceive as to its substantive moderation. And what I believe ought to be stressed in the case of radical humanism is the idea of *criticism* involved centrally in it, the 'Faustian' spirit of everlasting negation, i.e. pure transcendence but only – so far as it goes – in thought, in the realm proper to spirit. Criticism blows hot and cold at the same time, depending on its target. Virtue, happiness and criticism thus together make up the conceptual milieu of this early phase of European radical and socialist thought, a rather uneasy triad of goals, values and ideas, bequeathed to its most illustrious offspring, Marxism.

There is yet another way in which to characterize early socialism, still in general terms but now paying more attention to what many people would regard as 'tangible' or 'secular' historical factors. It will, of course, have been noticed that throughout these lectures I have shown only an intermittent interest in 'real' history: concrete events, institutional changes, the development of social forces, etc. Partly this stems from a desire to avoid either implicitly accepting or peremptorily dismissing the Marxist account of history, which is of course cast in predominantly 'materialistic' terms. I have made it clear from the beginning that my conscious aim in these four lectures is to make the genesis of Marxism intelligible, as distinguished from passing definitive verdicts on Marx's particular theories. For the former purpose – though probably not for the latter – it seems to me sufficient to treat our subject as one falling strictly within the *history of ideas*. However, from time to time – and this is certainly one such occasion – 'secular' history deserves an emphatic, albeit brief, mention. Early socialism is certainly unintelligible without reference to the cataclysm of the French Revolution of 1789 and its aftermath. To put the point succinctly (and not minding very much the commonplace involved), this tremendous event, coming in the wake of the Enlightenment and (it seems) irreversibly changing the nature of political power and authority in Europe, and the relationship of social and other groupings, raised sky-high the expectations of radically-minded writers and activists who were hoping, wishing and working for the revolutionary process to go on until the attainment of perfection: a society of freedom, equality, brotherhood, virtue and happiness. These expectations were dashed. The revolution, after decades of turmoil, settled in what Marx would call the 'bourgeois' mould, with paradigmatic liberalism triumphant, flanked by modern conservatism on its Right and democratic nationalism on its Left. Whither from here? Socialists of all kinds were obviously intent, in some sense, to 'continue' the revolution thus prematurely arrested, or dislocated, but what seems to make an interesting difference in our context is their actual *departure*. It was possible, broadly speaking, to latch on to the modern liberal settlement itself, as a whole, and proceed from this base directly and more or less smoothly; or it was possible to fasten on to the brief but heady *climax* of the revolution – the revolution in its purest phase, that which had itself been overturned by the 'settlement' – and continue from there; this of course implied a sharp break with the present. Utopian socialism and to an extent radical humanism follow the former road, revolutionary communism follows the latter. This historical divergence may also shed some light on the heterogeneity of the formation of Marxism, as alluded to in the foregoing.

        *   *   *

There is, as we remarked in the previous lecture, a certain kind of impelling 'logic' in the development of radical democracy to revolutionary communism. On the side of ideas, at any rate, communism is demonstrably the direct consequence of people 'taking equality seriously'. The culminating state of communism is reached, however, also as a result of secular political experience in the years of war, chaos and destruction around the turn of the century. Revolutionary communism emerges out of the embers of the great French Revolution almost as a 'necessity', given the values and goals of the purest form of Enlightenment radicalism. It is communism of *equals*, of people equal in moral worth as well as life-conditions; communism of *virtue*, the unity of people willing the common good; communism of *welfare*, proclaiming the community's responsibility for the well-being of individuals; and communism of mutual help and *co-operation*, looking forward to a society in which working for one another is seen and experienced by people not merely as a moral duty but also as a form of pleasure. And it is also communism of *struggle*, predicated on the need to stamp out mercilessly all kinds of social evil, and human reprobateness, including the physical liquidation of opponents. Virtue is borne of blood.

The revolutionary decades in Europe, and of course especially in France, supply both negative and positive lessons in teaching the necessity as well as reasonableness of communism. The negative aspects of revolutionary experience are more obvious and better known: the old and implacable enemies of the revolution, aristocrats, émigrés, foreign interests, are still around and threatening; the split between the moderate and radical wings of revolutionary forces is becoming more and more visible, with a decisive *halt* to the revolutionary process, symbolized in the coup of 9th Thermidor and the abrogation of the radical-democratic Jacobin Constitution of Year III, once again restricting the franchise. Also, the apathy of the people, especially in the countryside, and the hold of conservative sentiments over them, are noted with resentment and consternation, leading to a more resolute espousal of temporary dictatorship by the 'virtuous'. But there are also positive elements in the experience of revolution, pushing towards communism, perhaps not always appreciated in relevant historical accounts. Reference is here primarily to government and day-to-day administration in war-torn France and besieged Paris, necessitating a kind of 'war communism', with regimentation of labour, food rationing, and a centralized command structure. Babeuf himself, the original founder of revolutionary communism in modern times, having at first been involved in rural land administration in his native region, and active in the redistribution of agricultural estates among the poor peasantry, became an official with the Paris Food Administration under the Jacobin government in the 1790s. His experience there, so historians tell us, was decisive in confirming his egalitarian and communist convictions. Communism for him, that is to say, became not only a noble aim but also an immediate political necessity in preventing the continuation – and reappearance – of the distinction between rich and poor.

Perhaps this is the appropriate place to make the general point that revolutionary communism, in its early Left-Jacobin and Babouvist phase, was predominantly anti-aristocratic in orientation, preoccupied with the problem of *land*, intent on eliminating privileges, the extreme – and increasingly isolated – section of the great social and political movement towards the establishment of equality, liberty and popular government. In no sense was this communism 'modern' in the sense of being a *response* to capitalism; it could not have been, since capitalism (in the Marxist sense) had hardly got off the ground in France at this time. It represented no developed 'class' of industrial workers, but, at best, a collection of highly sophisticated and idealistic intellectuals, outcasts and desperadoes, destitute peasants and the urban 'rabble'. In its perspective the contrast between this advanced revolutionary 'élite' and the benighted rural masses was sharp; hence its anti-individualism, shrill militancy, impatient insurrectionism. Revolutionary communism is not, therefore, in any meaningful sense the 'heir' to modern liberalism but, figuratively speaking, its estranged half-brother, setting forth a deliberate and sharply opposed *alternative* to liberal values and concepts. This point is quite important in considering the nature of the Marxist synthesis: in as much as Marx's thought contains the major premise of revolutionary communism – in whatever disguise or adaptation – it contains an *atavism*, a stumbling-block in the full realization of the synthesis. And I would argue that this major premise – this incongruity – *is* present in Marxism, in the adoption of a stance of uncompromising 'class' militancy, in the advocacy of 'proletarian dictatorship', and in the concept of the 'communist party'.

Of course there is no question of the egalitarian communism of Francois-Noel 'Gracchus' Babeuf entering into Marxism directly. Marx's well-known contemptuous dismissal of 'crude communism' in the *Manuscripts* (and in some passages of *The Holy Family*, written jointly with Engels) as well as his scattered substantive references to his own vision of communism are enough evidence to show that he had scant regard for some of the *values* of egalitarian communism. Not for Marx the levelling down, the puritanism, the prejudice against diversity and intellectual achievement. But I think it is a different question when one considers other aspects of revolutionary communism, namely its built-in sharp dichotomy of rich and poor, or class conflict, and its advocacy of temporary educational dictatorship by the revolutionary élite. This side of the egalitarian heritage finds its way into Marxist doctrine through the impact of *Blanquism*. Now again we have to be careful: although Babeuf and Blanqui are often mentioned in conjunction in histories of socialism, the thread between them is the 'logic of ideas' rather than any personal influence or conscious adaptation. Blanqui, it is surmised, may have known personally Philippe Buonarotti, historian of Babouvism and the most famous survivor of the Conspiracy of Equals. But he does not refer to either of them in his theoretical writings and indeed on one occasion he disclaimed Babouvism in an interview.

Yet Louis Auguste Blanqui, veteran insurrectionist and charismatic leader, is undoubtedly the chief transmitter of this 'hard line' in modern socialism, the link between Rousseauist radical democracy, leftwing Jacobinism, egalitarian communism and Marxism. An archetypal model of the 'professional revolutionary', Blanqui spent thirty-three years of his life in prison for political offences, yet died in 1881, at the age of seventy-six, a free man. If, it has been said, he had not happened to be 'inside' during the Paris Commune of 1871, history might have taken a different turn. He was fanatical and devoted, a lifelong teetotaller and vegetarian. Of his ideas, three should be highlighted in our present context. Firstly, Blanqui was a firm intransigent atheist who considered religious belief to be incompatible with human independence and dignity – a view clearly derived from eighteenth-century French materialism and at the same time representing a distant echo of an older European tradition of secular and scientific thought, the one we identified earlier as the perspective of understanding. Militant atheism, as we shall see later, was taken for granted by Marx who considered the principle to be a necessary presupposition in the process leading to the attainment of 'practical atheism', i.e. full communist consciousness and society. Secondly, Blanqui had an out-and-out conflictual view of history, seeing history as the permanent arena of the war between classes, the struggle between rich and poor, oppressors and the oppressed. He believed that this conflict was irreconcilable and the oppressed had no choice but to wage the war relentlessly, to the point of complete victory; there was no compromise, no 'third way.' Again, this harsh and chilling view of the relationship of classes in modern society is a clear hallmark of Marxist socialism, distinguishing it from 'utopian' and similar departures. Thirdly, Blanqui was adamant that the oppressed could achieve victory

only through armed struggle, an insurrection led by the enlightened revolutionary vanguard. The mass of the people were not
yet ready to take on the enemy without this leadership. It was
therefore reasonable for 'intellect' to lead the way; intellectuals
and workers, Blanqui considered, brain and brawn, were natural
allies, in the same camp.

Concerning this last point, obviously it would be untrue to
say that Marxism takes on the mantle of Blanquism, in a pure
and simple fashion; Marx was certainly not an 'insurrectionist'.
But neither would it be entirely true to say that Marxism is
wholly free of Blanqist influence and affinity. The relationship
between Blanqui and Marx is highly complex, at all levels,
political, personal and theoretical. Marx never met Blanqui in
person, although his son-in-law, Paul Lafargue, once invited
Blanqui to London. But Marx clearly respected Blanqui, and
was impressed by him; he regarded Blanqui as the 'head and
heart of the proletarian party in France', the standard-bearer of
revolutionary communism in its fight against all kinds of utopians and compromisers. Marx's revolutionary comrades, like
him political exiles from Germany, were in the 1830s and 1840s
close associates of Blanqui in various insurrectionary ventures.
German Blanquists were co-founders of the Communist
League, which before Marx's accession was itself essentially a
conspiratorial and insurrectionist revolutionary organization.
There is, in the famous section of the *Communist Manifesto*
devoted to a scathing critique of all kinds of non-revolutionary
socialism, no critical mention of Blanqui's ideas or movement;
it seems to me clear therefore that in this period at any rate, in
the heady days of 1848–9, Marx identified himself with the line
of revolutionary communism chiefly represented by Blanqui.
The Marxist definition of the communist party as an élite, the
'most advanced section' of the working class, is also to be
found in the *Manifesto*. The phrase, the 'dictatorship of the
proletariat', used by Marx very sparingly, also surfaces around
this time, and it definitely connects up with Blanquism. Of
course Marx 'grew out' of Blanquism later, as the failure of
revolution in the mid-century pushed him more in the direction
of social science, and therewith to scientific socialism and attendant political circumspection and relative moderation. Marxists

and Blanquists clashed in radical politics in the latter half of the century. But it is interesting to note – again suggesting deep affinity – that Blanquism itself also 'grew out' of insurrectionist élitism in due course. Having learnt from his failures, Blanqui later formed a Revolutionary Socialist Party which had a large and respectable membership, not confined to activists; this party fused with the Marxists in 1901 to form the Socialist Party of France (becoming the mighty SFIO in 1905).

In digressing a bit, we might make here the point briefly that the charge of 'Blanquism' later levelled at Lenin by mainstream 'scientific' Marxists (e.g. Plekhanov, Kautsky) appears to be fundamentally misconceived, in that it assumes a *sharp* break between Blanqui and Marx. It is true that Lenin directly absorbed the ideas of Tkachev, famous Russian exile and admirer of Blanqui, and *maybe* Marx would not have been entirely happy with the content and tone of Lenin's intransigent statements in *What Is To Be Done* and similar texts. But this consideration overlooks the fact that the 'red thread' of revolutionary communism, of Blanquism, is deeply woven into the texture of Marxism and can be extricated only at the expense of removing, so to speak, the biting sting of Marxist doctrine: its hard aggression, its menacing revolutionary momentum and ethos. Lenin I think could legitimately appeal to *this* thread in Marx's thought, as other Marxist leaders and writers could invoke other threads. Marxism is complex and heterogeneous in a disturbing but also an exciting and fertile way: all 'logics', including the ironclad logic of revolutionary communism, are detectable in it. The red revolutionary thread of Marxism, highlighting such central and distinctive features as irreconcilable class antagonism in history, the need for uncompromising militancy and revolutionary 'class consciousness' in the proletariat, the preparation for a necessary phase of disruption and armed struggle, the identification of a leading élite within the working class, the alliance of intellectuals and workers, dictatorship envisaged for the transition period after the revolution, and last but not least the ideal of comradely partnership in a future communist society of *workers*, comes from this background and no other. Without this element Marxism would unquestionably have been swallowed up in 'mechanistic' social science and/or ineffectual 'criticism'. The doctrine of revolution does *not* come either from radical political economy or from philosophical humanism; it enlivens and fertilizes both. Through Marx's revolutionary ideas therefore we gain a clear glimpse of Blanqui's militant élitism as well as Babeuf's virtuous egalitarianism, and through these a retrospective vista back to the tradition of radical democracy as an integral part of the European Enlightenment.

I may be permitted to conclude this section by advancing a couple of highly speculative – but I think relevant – remarks on the substantive, theoretical importance of the ideas of revolutionary communism for Marxism. Crude and disturbing though they may be, neither élitist 'leadership' nor virtuous 'equality' can simply be dismissed out of hand. Taking the doctrine of leadership first: if socialism or communism *really* means the creation of a new world, a veritable transcendence of the present, of 'actual existence', then what is clearly required is a *very* 'cool look' indeed at what is going on. What is going on, clearly, is that the mass of the 'oppressed' are actively contributing to their oppression, by meekly acquiescing, by being successfully duped, by having a 'false consciousness'. It would be simply inconceivable to understand oppression in any other way. It follows, therefore, that the masses must initially be *exploded* out of their torpor by a 'shock', which in turn means accepting the heavy responsibility of leadership, the task of actually rousing popular consciousness, or supplying the 'detonator'. There are many ways of inducing the shock but élitist 'temporary' dictatorship by advanced revolutionaries is by far the easiest, the most obvious and advantageous. Very few successful Marxist leaders and movements have got away from this pure logic of revolution in theory, and even fewer in practice. That the same logic causes well-nigh intractable problems for Marxist *establishments* (i.e. the 'bureaucratization' of leadership) is of course to be noted but it is not our concern here. And now taking the doctrine of equality, in the strong, Babouvist sense: is there really an alternative to its pursuit in principle, once the transcendence of present existence and the realization of communism are the declared aims? It is deceptively easy to discard pure egalitarianism as 'levelling down' or 'uniformity'.

But what *is* equality in the last resort if not uniformity or at least a process towards the attainment of uniformity? Without people feeling the same as others, which means *being* the same as others, communism in the full sense cannot be realized. Equality of moral worth, of need, of merit, of consideration, etc. are nothing but empty and inconsequential rhetoric which are all perfectly compatible with the 'formal' equality enshrined in liberalism and which socialists and communists set out to combat in the first place. Anything short of substantive equality, i.e. uniformity, will *always* lead to the return of distinctions, asymmetries, power-differentials, open or hidden privileges. What I am trying to suggest here is that Marx's 'transcendence' of 'crude' egalitarianism *à la* Babeuf may in fact have weakened the perspective of *transcendence* in Marxism itself, thereby diluting its pure revolutionary appeal as well as – like leadership degenerating into bureaucracy – bringing into sharp relief the coherence and veracity of its promises.

＊　　＊　　＊

But let us now turn to the second big chunk figuring in the formation of Marxism, and providing, if you like, one of those 'diluting' factors and influences referred to above. I propose to discuss this under the general heading of 'utopian socialism', though this does mean employing the 'utopian' tag in a considerably wider sense than encountered in general parlance and the exegetical literature. But there are good reasons for adopting this procedure. The common and accepted meaning of 'utopian', I take it (and it would be tedious to go into the etymology of the word), is a person who dreams up and describes in detail a fictitious society where everything is perfect and everybody is happy, or a piece of writing that contains such a description. Utopians are said to believe that these ideal societies are in fact attainable, and hence their descriptions can and should also serve as 'blueprints'. The strong, added connotation of the word is that utopians are mistaken in this belief; therefore their blueprints are useless (they might be interesting *literature* though). I hasten to add that although this pejorative connotation is quite common, it is by no means universally shared, a point which is relevant to a discussion of Marxism – as I shall explain in the closing section of this lecture.

Now it is certainly true that Marx and Engels in their numerous statements concerning utopian socialism adhered to this commonly accepted meaning, together with its pejorative connotation. Marx looked down on and rejected utopian departures; to them he contrasted his own understanding of socialism, which was both 'revolutionary' and 'scientific'; utopian socialism was neither. This already gives us a clue as to the way in which the meaning of 'utopian' has to be extended for the purposes of our discussion. The point to make is that the above-mentioned general meaning of utopianism, although present, is not really very prominent in the Marxist critical perspective. Instead, I think, the following features attributed by Marx to utopian socialism should be emphasized here. Firstly, utopian socialism is piecemeal socialism, envisaging a gradual process of change from actual to ideal, starting from the bottom, from 'society', from individual attitudes and lifestyles. There is no 'big bang' of revolution, no 'shock' administered by an advanced élite. Secondly, it signifies peaceful socialism: the way and the aim are both eminently 'rational' and desirable for all concerned. Every sane person can and will be persuaded of the superiority of the new society over the old one; socialism is in everybody's best 'interest'. This peaceful aspect ties up closely with the piecemeal aspect: the best way to propagate socialism is by living it, through the attractive example of those – individuals and small groups – who have already effected the change in their consciousness, activities and relationships. Thirdly, utopian socialism is paternal and familial in its perspective, focusing on the 'people' in general, men and women of good will and natural desires, rather than on definite groups in society. That is to say, while the writers usually considered under this label were not oblivious of the existence of classes or of the conflict between them, they did not regard socialism as exclusively the affair of the working class or that an intensification of social conflict must precede political change or that the new society would actually *grow out* of the antagonistic development of classes. Hence, in the Marxist view at any rate, utopianism stops short of being 'revolutionary' for precisely the same reason as it fails in being 'scientific': blind to the dynamism – or dialectic – of the present, it has no clear view of a future born (necessarily) of present conflict either. In the terse Marxist expression utopian socialism is 'immature'.

Beyond these general features, however, utopian socialism would defy any description as a distinctive political 'doctrine'. Utopian movements – small groups of like-minded people setting up and running experimental 'communities' – had a great deal in common in terms of their cherished values and preferred modes of action, but the same would not be true as regards their respective social philosophies. The difference between the perspectives of Saint-Simon, Fourier, Owen, Cabet and Weitling (just to mention those most frequently referred to in the literature) is sometimes almost as large and conspicuous as their collective distance from the perspective of Marxism. It follows, therefore, that in examining the role – if any – of utopian socialism in the formation of Marxism one has to adopt a discerning attitude; it can, I think, be taken for granted that any meaningful connection will be found on the plane of *ideas*, rather than in the field of practical politics. On the other hand, defining utopian socialism thus widely: as 'piecemeal–peaceful– paternal', will enable us to operate on a larger canvas, taking into our purview other relevant contemporary departures which might not necessarily appear 'utopian' in the more customary, narrower sense. I shall thus, in the ensuing paragraphs, make some brief comment on Saint-Simonism, Fourierism, Owenism, and so-called 'Ricardian socialism'.

All these four departures, though in varying degrees and senses, can be seen as direct emanations of the Enlightenment and mainstream liberalism which they intend to carry further. This is in sharp and relevant contrast to revolutionary communism which, as we have seen, in spite of its strident modernity harks essentially back to the pristine democratic elements of liberalism in the latter's earliest infancy. The Enlightenment and liberal stamp is most conspicuous in the case of Saint-Simonian doctrine. As regards the founder himself, Henri Comte de Saint-Simon (1760–1825), the 'socialist' character of this doctrine is in some doubt, implicit rather than openly set out; though with some of the best and most influential disciples of Saint-Simon socialism definitely comes to the fore. The gist, it seems to me, of Saint-Simonism is its emphasis on social organization for the promotion of wealth-creation. Dreamer and schemer rolled into one and the archetypal 'rationalist', Saint-Simon put forward an exciting theory of history, scattered in numerous pamphlets and articles, which designated the nineteenth century as a new 'organic period', after the 'critical' eighteenth century, confronted with the task of scientific social construction. As in medieval Europe, the new society would be governed by 'spiritual' and 'temporal' leaders. However, the modern world is based on *science*, not religion. A 'Council of Newton' is to take over from the Vatican and harness all human energies to the conquest of nature and the creation of the material prerequisites of general happiness. The realm of physics – knowledge of external nature – is to be extended to the realm of morality and human conduct – 'social physics' – based on the Newtonian universal 'law of gravity'. A 'new Christianity' is to inculcate an ethic of work, rational enjoyment and social responsibility.

While scientists are the spiritual leaders of society, temporal direction is to be undertaken by *producers*, i.e. people whose efforts are generally useful to the well-being of society and who translate scientific knowledge into the actual subjugation of nature. Saint-Simon draws a fundamental distinction – novel as well as influential – between 'industrialists' and 'idlers', those who promote the wealth of society and those who simply waste it. The latter include, predictably, aristocrats, church dignitaries, politicians and all kinds of civil servants. The former group, and this is an interesting point, has reference to the 'captains' of industry as well as its army of ordinary working privates. Where, in other words, Saint-Simon notes a basic conflict of interest, it is between the historical and social principles of aristocratic and of bourgeois predominance; the bourgeois world for him is *the* modern world, still progressive but it needs *organization* to fulfil its potential. The category of 'industrials' contains no basic internal conflict of interest; productive owners of natural resources, and above all bankers, are the properly appointed superiors and commanders of the army of production. There is no social equality in Saint-Simon's ideal world; but there is fairness, expert leadership, harmony and of course happiness.

We are only a tiny step away from socialism to which the 'logic' of Saint-Simon's rationalistic doctrine definitely tends (though it did lead in other directions, too, as witness Auguste Comte's conservative-oriented science of 'sociology', for instance). Rodriguez, Leroux and most importantly Bazard, in his famous lectures in Paris in the 1820s, drew explicitly socialist conclusions from the master's teaching. Programmatic epitomes of socialism, occurring also in Marxist texts, like the aim of replacing the exploitation of man by man with the joint human exploitation of nature, and the principle, 'from each according to his capacity, to each according to his work', saw their original formulation in Saint-Simonism. The move towards socialism, on Saint-Simonian grounds, was indeed sensible: if wealth-creation is the central aim of society, if production and 'industry' are to be extolled and idleness and wastage to be eliminated, if the new social ethic of general welfare is to be seriously promoted, and if scientific knowledge is to provide the principles and methods of government, then certain historically entrenched institutions, like private property, are at one point bound to reveal themselves as *obsolete*, detrimental to further progress. Thus Bazard, arguing from these rationalistic Saint-Simonian premises, came to question the justification and sense of private inheritance. He also looked forward to the public ownership of land and capital. We do have here then the foundations – or at least *one* foundation – of Marxist 'scientific socialism', the vision of a society geared to the maximization of production, of wealth-creation in the service of general human happiness, a world from which all 'idlers' have disappeared. Note that – in spite of the glowing rhetoric – this is a *pedestrian* kind of socialism which, in terms of human aims and values, scarcely if at all 'transcends' the ethos of bourgeois liberalism (while, as it were, it calls the bluff of liberalism: if liberal *values* are to triumph, liberal *institutions* must be superseded); it is also a decidedly *worldly* and *cool* approach to socialism, enlightened and scientific in spirit, stressing both productive efficiency and consumer satisfaction, organization and leadership, welfare and material plenty. Saint-Simonism is directly echoed in Stalinism as well as, at the other extreme, in Swedish social democracy.

This liberal and coolly rationalistic core of Saint-Simonian thought, however, sharply contrasts to Saint-Simonian 'religion' and utopian experimentation – more in the public eye at the time. With Charles Fourier, whose name is often coupled with Saint-Simon's, things are rather different. Fourier is difficult, or perhaps impossible, to classify: the paradigmatic 'utopian' thinker whose flights of fantasy are unmatched, whose metaphysics and cosmology radically depart from the path of Enlightenment, who excels in the devising of detailed 'blueprints' and whose practical suggestions and influence are closely linked to his philosophy (unlike Saint-Simonism) – but whose 'socialism', to say the least, is problematic. Fourier's radicalism both exceeds that of Marx and falls short of it; the Fourierist influence on Marx is marginal and negligible; the importance of Fourier in our context lies in his stance being *complementary* to Marxism, highlighting perhaps some of the shortcomings of the latter. The gist of Fourier's message, as it appears, is the attainment of happiness and the perfect society through the complete satisfaction of the basic human 'passions'. Bitterly critical of modern civilization (including Enlightenment rationalism), with particular reference to the waste and immorality of commerce and the unnatural restraint on passions by the institution of marriage, Fourier advocated the immediate establishment – which he believed was possible through peaceful persuasion and the assistance of sympathetic 'benefactors' – of small, self-governing communities whose members were 'matched' in terms of their dominant 'passions'. The application of his great discovery, as he thought, the 'law of passionate attraction', would remedy all social ills.

Fourier describes in minute and fascinating detail life in these communities or 'phalanxes', including furniture and culinary customs. Very elaborate organization, in his scheme, is to serve the free and total unfolding of the passionate nature of human beings. In telling contrast to Saint-Simon, Fourier turns away from industry and economic expansion: in his phalanxes simple agricultural pursuits prevail (a loner himself, he was very fond of cats and flowers). Two aspects of phalanx-life are especially worthy of attention. Firstly, Fourier believes himself able to solve the age-old problem of drudgery, i.e. labouring, by completely abolishing the division of labour and professionalization:

people in the phalanxes move around all the time, from one kind of 'work' to another; thus life for them is continuous excitement, novelty. Most famous, perhaps, is Fourier's quite ingenious assignment of dirty work to children who are naturally 'attracted' to slime and filth. Secondly, Fourier intends to allow, indeed encourage, the free flow of sexual passions in all directions, including those considered 'perversions' in civilization. His manuscripts, unpublished in his life-time, contain very interesting descriptions indeed of the orgiastic festivals of the phalanxes, with matching encounters of people with diverse 'manias' carefully organized by specially appointed sexual experts. Yet on the other hand Fourier's phalanxes do not eliminate private property, profit-making and factional intrigue, the thinker recognizing the legitimacy of the 'cabalist' passion among others. Thus once again, when layers of fantasy and rhetoric are peeled away, the 'utopian' community of the phalanx is revealed as being not *too* dissimilar from certain basic features and developmental tendencies found in modern 'civilization' – more visible, of course, in our times than in Fourier's.

I would argue that the Fourierist impact on Marxism is negligible and that Marx is better to be seen as a *contrast* to Fourier than his 'successor'. Engels, it is true, does make the point somewhere that Fourier's critique of modern commerce was influential in the early formation of Marxist thought. But, correct though this may be on a certain level, the basis of the Marxist perspective on this – I think much more profound and impressive than Fourier's – has a different origin, viz. in Marx's theory of the alienation of labour, which we shall of course look at more closely at the appropriate place. There is of course *one* single sentence in the Marxist corpus (in *The German Ideology*, published posthumously), about people fishing in the afternoon, criticizing after dinner, etc. in 'communist society', quoted right, left and centre in the exegetical literature, which does bear the unmistakable imprint of Fourier. But although Marx continued to pay lip-service to the notion of the 'abolition of the division of labour' in communism, it is obvious that his heavily industrial, expansionist and organizational scenario, while pretty close to Saint-Simonism, is quite incompatible with Fourier's bucolic vision of labour as 'play' (as Marx himself contemptuously puts it in another posthumously published manuscript).

Which leaves the point about Fourierism as being 'complementary' and indeed perhaps a 'corrective' to Marxism. I would simply like to advance two considerations here, one being probably more obvious than the other. In the first place Fourier's concentration on individual psychology, on basic 'passions', and his resultant *libertarian* perspective, do chart a territory which, at best, is sorely neglected in Marx's writings, and at worst had its legitimacy as such denied by implication. Sex is not the only example but the most conspicuous one. Though certainly 'progressive' in their views on sex – by Victorian standards – Marx and Engels do not put human sexuality, its problems, its repression, its 'liberation', in the centre of their theories. Man (including woman) for Marx is primarily a *labouring* animal, a *rational* animal, rather than a sexual animal. In this respect, if you like, Marxism is still 'pre-modern', its foundations squarely rooted in the liberal Enlightenment, preceding the Nietzschean and Freudian 'revolutions'. Whereas Fourier paradoxically, in contrast to his political and economic conservatism, not to mention his hair-raising historical and cosmological speculations, stands revealed as a thoroughly *modern* thinker, the daring early advocate of the liberation of passions and emotions, the forerunner of 'sexual radicalism' in all its important manifestations (e.g. radical feminism, gay liberation, the 'therapeutic' advocacy of uncensored pornography, etc.). To the extent that – in the twentieth century – a number of more or less successful attempts have been made to incorporate sexual radicalism into Marxism, both theory and practice, these should be seen as belated and backhanded apologies to Charles Fourier, the immature 'utopian dreamer'. I will leave the question open as to whether sexual radicalism – in contrast to original Marxism – is *really* 'radical' and 'revolutionary' or not. Clearly, there are telling arguments on either side.

This, however, raises another question, more elementary in a way but quite important for a proper appreciation of a fundamental problem built into Marxism. The Marx–Fourier contrast, as set out here, might help bring this problem into proper focus. To put it simply, Fourier intends to change society radically, and to revalue and reinterpret our ideas about society, in order to fit social arrangements to human beings *as they are*. Marx, on the other hand, looking upon human nature as an historical product, expects and works for a radical change in both – in society and in human beings – taking place simultaneously. There is little doubt that the Marxist conception is the more exciting, more intellectually sophisticated of the two. However, whatever we might think of the validity of the *particular* view of human nature advanced by Fourier – 'passionate attraction' and all that – we ought, I think, to consider the basic principle involved in Fourier's departure with some sympathy. We can ask the question: which of the two stances is more realistic, more commonsensical, of greater immediate use to the practical reformer? Could one not reasonably suggest that Marx, and especially his latter-day disciples – Marxist leaders in power – would have saved a lot of effort and sacrifices and blood (their own and that of those subject to their control) if they had proceeded on this pedestrian and 'utopian' principle, taking people as they were and expecting them to continue in their old individual ways on the morrow of the revolution? Again, the extent to which they have done so – against their intellectual convictions – demonstrates the residual *sense* of utopian socialism, so contemptuously discarded at the time.

Moving from Fourier to Owen and early British socialism is like leaving a Greek Orthodox church and entering into a Methodist meeting hall: the ideas encountered here are clear, simple, sensible, with none of the flamboyance surrounding the worlds of Saint-Simon and Fourier. The image seems appropriate, since it could truly be said that while one leg of Owenism is in classical political economy, the other is in the Protestant and Puritan tradition, 'secularized' of course some time earlier, as we remarked in the first lecture. (The word 'secular', incidentally, seems to have been coined by one of Owen's disciples.) The main significance of Robert Owen is not as a 'man of ideas' but as a man of affairs: gifted and successful entrepreneur, leader and inspirer, the founder of thriving (though only temporarily) co-operative communities on both sides of the Atlantic, the patron saint of native British socialism. The basis of Owen's thought, however, is found unmistakably in mainstream European liberalism, the values of which he adapts and carries forward; in originality he is not a match for either of the other two utopian founders discussed here. A latter-day eighteenth century *philosophe* in spirit, though with a marked philanthropic streak, Owen's big idea is the malleability of human character, through sound 'rational' education, wise leadership and appropriate social conditions, like improved housing, health and a humane work environment. A convinced utilitarian, like his one-time associate, the liberal philosopher Jeremy Bentham, Owen's aim is the greatest happiness of the greatest number, which at first he seeks to achieve by persuasion and force of example, appealing to his fellow entrepreneurs to treat their workers decently and thereby to change their character (i.e. get them off drink and promiscuity) – thus the manufacturer's profit will begin to rise! He moves from the position of 'welfare capitalism' largely as a result of external circmstances, viz. the hostility and indifference shown towards his benevolent schemes. Owen then turns more directly to the workers, becomes a leader in the budding trade union movement, and embraces 'co-operative' socialism. He is probably most famous, in this later stage, for his advocacy of the 'parallelogramms', i.e. village co-operative communities where production is for use, not for profit, and goods are exchanged by means of 'labour notes'. His ideas also harden somewhat, as he now takes cognizance of a conflict of interest between manufacturers and workers, and the growing gap between wealth and poverty resulting from the Industrial Revolution – but, remaining a rationalist at heart, he stops short of revolution. However, most significantly in our context, Owen is among those of the early socialists in Britain who embrace, and carry forward, the central idea of the liberal political economists, viz. the *labour theory of value*.

We left off political economy in the previous lecture, making one or two brief comments *à propos*, mainly, Adam Smith. It will be convenient to continue with this story here, since – as the point was made earlier – early socialists in Britain could broadly be classified under the 'utopian' label (with a few notable exceptions, of course). Like Owen, the radical followers of Smith and Ricardo started out from the concept of labour as the creator of wealth; some of them followed Owen in practical politics and supported the co-operative movement. David

Ricardo, last of the great classical political economists whom Marx honoured with the epithet 'scientist' (successors were dubbed 'hired prize-fighters of the bourgeoisie'), further developed and sharpened Smith's theory of value. Apart from technical improvements in the science of political economy, I think Ricardo's interest here attaches mainly to three things, all highlighting his *negative* significance in the formation of socialist doctrine in Britain, and leading also to Marxism (which, in its social scientific aspect, can reasonably be regarded as a 'British' doctrine, too). Firstly, with Ricardo the class conflict between the landowning aristocracy and new manufacturing and capitalist interests comes emphatically to the fore: Ricardo, more or less, condemns 'rent' as a form of unearned revenue, while upholding 'profit'. In his perspective capital and labour are, as it were, in an 'action alliance' against the class of landowners (the scene is the bitter controversies on the Corn Laws). Secondly, for Ricardo distribution, not production, is the central concern of political economy, and hence he makes no bones about *conflict* being endemic in capitalism; in the last analysis, profit and wage also stand in a 'zero-sum' relationship. And thirdly, with Ricardo's deadpan approach political economy is now revealed as the 'dismal science' (in sharp contrast to Adam Smith's serene optimism); in basic agreement with the gloomy scenario of Malthus's *Essay on Population*, Ricardo envisages continuing poverty and misery for the mass of wage-earners.

Here then was a glaring contradiction, noted and stressed in the liberals' own science of political economy itself. On the one hand, political economy acknowledged the primary significance of human labour in the creation of wealth. It asserted, on the other hand, that labour could *not* – in terms of the unalterable 'natural' laws of production and distribution – ever expect more than a marginal share of this wealth. The so-called 'Ricardian socialists' – a sample of radical writers who took classical political economy seriously and who drew radical conclusions from mainstream liberal premises – set out to resolve this contradiction. It was they who gave a moralistic twist to political economy, by moving a step further from Smith's morally ambiguous (i.e. 'detached') stance on labour as the sole 'measure' of value to the unambiguous assertion that labour is the sole *source* of value. Labour, therefore, they argued in so many ways, deserved its 'fair share', which in practice meant radical changes in the prevailing system of free enterprise economy. But the Ricardian socialists were not a 'group' or 'movement', and writers usually considered under this heading widely differed among themselves as to what was precisely the fault with capitalism and how much change was required in order to 'emancipate' labour. Thomas Hodgskin, for example, while in his exposition of the production process under capitalism anticipating Marx in many interesting ways, does not go much further than the advocacy of 'combination' for workers, so that labour may have a stronger bargaining position *vis-à-vis* capital. This is a doctrine of trade union militancy, one might say, rather than socialism. William Thompson, again, more radical than Hodgskin in his critique of the whole liberal ethos (e.g. competition, acquisitiveness), does not accept any class struggle as his starting-point but wants labour and capital to unite; he is a staunch supporter of Owenite co-operation (and of feminine emancipation). The American printer resident in Leeds in the 1830s, John Francis Bray, is probably the most radical of the Ricardian socialists (and, in my personal opinion, the best writer). His *Labour's Wrong and Labour's Remedy* (1839) is a little classic of early socialist literature. Bray's critique of capitalist society is thoroughgoing and his declared aim is full 'communism'. But his strategy nevertheless conforms to 'utopianism' in the broad sense employed here: he believes in the efficacy of gradual persuasion and example, a 'joint-stock company' which will spread and eventually embrace the whole country.

In a sense we might say then that the Ricardian socialists – in their understanding and critique of capitalism at any rate – almost reach the threshold of Marxism. Their formulations, using the terms and concepts derived from classical economy, prefigure Marxist arguments: the same 'bricks', as it were, go into the building of the humble cottages of these early socialists as are used in the construction of Marx's mighty and haughty palace. Also, it could be argued that the Ricardian socialists have a more 'advanced' standpoint than the revolutionary communists in France, in that they directly confront *capitalism* in full swing, i.e. a strong and emancipated bourgeoisie, and hence gain a glimpse of a proletarian *class* interest pitted against capitalism in its prevailing form – rather than confronting a tottering semi-aristocratic society and representing the 'poor' and 'oppressed' in general. However, by the same token it should be said that this early English socialism, from Owen to Bray – precisely because it arises in the context of victorious liberalism – cannot free itself from the basic *conceptual world* of liberalism. Hence it belittles the importance of class *struggle* and advocates 'co-operation' (in a variety of ways) instead of revolution. There is yet another way in which the 'moralistic' perspective of Ricardian socialism (and utopian socialism in general) can be characterized, and at the same time the dimensional move brought into socialist doctrine by Marx more clearly appreciated. The former does match, in almost all essentials, the Marxist understanding of labour, as the source of value. It does not match Marx's understanding of capital, as congealed labour, and hence as dynamic force, itself a vital factor in the revolutionization of production, leading beyond the capitalist system. Thus the Ricardian socialists can posit socialism as a *desirable* goal only, as a moral imperative, rather than as a *necessary* outcome of capitalist progress.

It is clear that Marx did not learn anything very important from the Ricardian socialists, as he undoubtedly did learn a great deal from Smith (mainly) and Ricardo. Among early English socialists and radicals only Owen gets a brief mention in Marx's *Paris Manuscripts*, and that is in connection with 'atheism' and not the labour theory of value (whereas the *Manuscripts* contain a hefty amount of documentation from Smith). Biographers of Marx have made the point that Marx first got to know the Ricardian socialists in 1845, that is, after the formulation of his own distinctive standpoint in the *Manuscripts*. Thereafter one finds a lot of references to them scattered all over the Marxist corpus, generally unflattering, at times even unfair. It is of relevance to note here – as being, in a way, marginally supportive evidence for the interpretation of Marxism ventured in these pages – that Marx is much more complimentary in his attitude towards the 'bourgeois' giants – Smith, Hegel, Ricardo – than towards his immediate predecessors in the radical camp or contemporary socialists, like Feuerbach, Owen, the Ricardian socialists and Proudhon. It is in his contemptuous attack on Proudhon in *The Poverty of Philosophy* that Marx devotes also a few pages to a merciless demolition of Bray's 'exchange utopia'. *Theories of Surplus Value* contains likewise a number of asides on Hodgskin, critical in the main. For Marx, it appears, it was much more important for someone to have his head screwed on the right way than to have his heart in the proper place.

To conclude then on utopian socialism, its significance in the formation of Marxism is considerable, though not overwhelming. A brief mention has already been made concerning the utopian critique of capitalist society and bourgeois-liberal values, which Marx 'develops', though, as we suggested, he largely goes his own independent way, attaching his criticism of the capitalist order to the concept of alienation. Marx's science of political economy has little to do with utopian socialism, as we have just seen. However, it might be suggested that certain elements found in utopian socialist writing make an appearance as aspects of the Marxist *vision* of future communist society, putting as it were flesh on the bones, filling out gaps, adding some illustrative detail to what would otherwise be a highly abstract scenario. Communism in Marx, that is to say, refers to a society where production is efficiently *organized* (Saint-Simon), where producers are freely and willingly *co-operating* (Owen), and where people are reasonably *happy* and *satisfied* (Fourier). The libertarian vision of Fourier is not, of course, fully accommodated in Marxism – it might indeed be suggested (as we have done earlier) that Fourier and Marx provide contrasting, rather than complementary, accounts of human nature and the society to come. Saint-Simon and Owen are much more 'at home' in Marx and their respective emphases on organization and co-operation seem to dovetail – are 'synthesized' – in the Marxist perspective. Taking a fairly big jump here, we could perhaps surmise that some underlying problems encountered later in Marxist political *construction* can be traced back to the discrepancy – maybe incompatibility – between the Sain-Simonian and Owenite visions, indicating that they were not after all properly 'digested' by Marx. To put it summarily, organization requires leadership, hierarchy, a highly developed division of labour. Co-operation, on the other hand, implies decentralization and some sort of 'workers' control'. These two aspects of socialism will not smoothly co-exist just by virtue of someone (like Marx) *saying* that they will. Practice is different from theory. But we will return to this question – the coherence or otherwise of Marx's synthesis – at the end of this lecture, taking in the whole gamut of early socialism and radicalism, as making up the formation of Marx's thought.

*   *   *

In considering the development of German idealist thought in the radical and revolutionary direction – the third and last chunk to be noted in discussing the formation of Marxism – we must be mindful of two things. Firstly, the Left or 'Young' Hegelians were among Marx's teachers, friends, working colleagues during Marx's *personal* 'formative period' (which is of course not quite the same thing as the 'formation' of Marxist thought). Consequently Marx's relationship to them is much more intimate, familiar, than his relation to revolutionary communists and utopian socialists. In the earlier writings (as we shall see in the following lecture) Marx's main concerns as well as his language derive almost wholly from Left Hegelianism. At the same time – familiarity here, too, bred contempt – Marx's reaction to Left Hegelianism is considerably more violent and critical than his attitude to the other two strands. With the latter he could afford to be paternally dismissive; with the former it was necessary to be personally vituperative and at times cruelly contemptuous. Marx cuts his intellectual teeth on criticizing Hegel and his radical followers; his embracing of communism and political economy is simultaneously a conscious endeavour to liberate himself from Left Hegelian concerns and language. Secondly, the 'universe' in which Left Hegelian thought moves and operates is itself radically different from the milieu of the other two strands we have just seen. With both revolutionary communism and utopian socialism *worldly* and *practical* concerns are predominant; the formulation and propagation of ideas here are closely connected with the fortunes of actual political *movements*. Undoubtedly Left Hegelian radicals are also 'worldly' and 'practical' in their intentions but here the distinguishing mark is the attempt to realize worldly goals *through* thinking, through a thorough reinterpretation and transvaluation of, mainly, *religion* and *philosophy*. The starting-point is not so much, as with the others, the perceived facts of poverty, inequality, oppression and exploitation but rather a sense of intellectual frustration, of wanting to reveal the bare truth concealed beneath the transcendental language of Hegelian philosophy, the truth *in* Hegel but not fully noted and communicated *by* him. The Left Hegelian 'movement' was of course confined to a handful of highly sophisticated academics and journalists; its direct political impact was negligible.

The general point we made in the previous lecture about the 'presence' of Hegel in Marxism could be restated here, with almost (though not wholly) the same force of application. Hegel's presence in Marx, we argued, is *intensive* rather than *extensive*, it relates to an overriding concern and momentum, a guiding 'spirit', and not to concrete doctrinal formulations. Similarly, what Marx takes on – and what is of crucial significance in the formation of Marxism – is the Left Hegelian 'spirit' of intransigent *radical humanism*, the confidence of seeing the light beyond the mist of confusions, half-truths, distortions, the conviction that the only way to progress lies through the thorough 'digestion' (as opposed to discarding) of philosophy and religion. In pure thinking – the further 'soaring' of the soaring thought of modern liberalism, noted previously – Left Hegelianism of course far transcends the rather crude and pedestrian gropings of hard-headed communists, soft-hearted utopians and the modest epigoni of Smith and Ricardo. It is this 'soaring', this going the 'whole hog' of modern thought, this dimensional jump, which Marx takes in due course to his reading of political economy and communism and which, by providing the intellectual lynchpin of his 'synthesis', *lifts* his thought up above those of his immediate predecessors. Again, however, we must proceed with some caution. Throughout I have been stressing the importance of the European *mainstream* in the genesis of Marxism, attempting to put 'gestation' on a par with, if not slightly above, 'formation'. The modern foundations epitomized in Rousseau and Smith figure in this interpretation more weightily than the departures of Blanqui or

Saint-Simon. Likewise, the Left Hegelian contribution ought not to be overemphasized. In the deeper and final analysis, I would argue, Hegel counts for more than Bauer, Ruge, Hess or Feuerbach. Indeed – though this is strictly speaking not a part of our enterprise here, since it concerns the 'life', rather than the genesis, of Marxism – it could be said that Marx in his very maturity *returns* to Hegel (on a deep level) and consequently moves even further *away* from Left Hegelianism. Still, at the same time it must be acknowleged that Marx directly and literally *learnt* from the Left Hegelians – in a way that he could not be said to have 'learnt' anything from the French and the English – and thus the importance of the former is to be appreciated on this 'groundfloor' level also.

In the ensuing rather brief survey of the development of Left Hegelian thought, therefore, we should I think highlight the twin concerns of religion and philosophy, through the attempt – which seems to define Left Hegelianism as a whole – to 'translate' these into a programme of practical action and a radical change in human consciousness and social relations. Hegel 'left off', in a manner of speaking, with two dominant and (to his radical-minded students at any rate) disturbing ambiguities. He left, in the first place, religion in a limbo: philosophy 'transcends' religion but does it mean that religion is *confirmed* on its appropriate level (i.e. belief, observance, etc.) or does it mean that religion has now *lost* its meaning and is therefore to be abolished altogether, in thought as well as practice? And if it is the latter (which of course was the Left Hegelians' contention), then does this not lead in the end also necessarily to the dethronement of philosophy, as 'pure thought' and *quasi*-religion, and its translation into *practical* human concerns? In the second place, Hegel also left the future in limbo: truth for him is the sole preserve of philosophy –'absolute Spirit' – and philosophy is by its very nature retrospective, not predictive or even admonitory. The future is strictly, literally 'free': self-determining, unknowable. But could Hegel have seriously *meant* this? And if he did, is this not a serious flaw in his thought, a deep irrationality which has to be corrected and through that correction the Hegelian 'freedom of reason' brought to bear on the actual world? Left Hegelians proceeded by giving more and more resolutely affirmative answers to these questions, resolving Hegel's fertile ambiguity in the direction of militant humanism and practical, future-oriented worldliness. The two works which are usually regarded as the first landmarks in this development, Strauss' *Life of Jesus* (1835) and Cieszkowski's *Prolegomena to Historiosophy* (1838) can be seen as respectively charting out the paths to follow in the critical demolition and reinterpretation of religion and in the practical transformation of philosophy. Strauss, and following him Bruno Bauer (at one time Marx's friend and mentor), contend that the truth and meaning of Christianity lie in the intrinsic value of the human species as such; they attack the 'mythical' aspects of the Gospels and question the historicity of Jesus. Cieszkowski argues that philosophy must attend to the problem of the future; now that we know the ultimate truth from Hegel (though darkly) that *reason* is the highest in reality as regards human affairs, we must *act* in accordance with this 'revelation'. 'Praxis', action infused by philosophy, must now follow – the word 'praxis' was later enthusiastically picked up by the young Marx and has remained ever since a key term in the vocabulary of Marx's latter-day 'humanist' followers.

These two fundamental concerns: religion and the future, come together dramatically in the thought of the outstanding paradigmatic figure of Left Hegelianism, Ludwig Feuerbach (1804–72). Although these days scholars tend to question the extent of the Feuerbachian influence on Marx, Feuerbach must still be counted as representing, arguably, the most decisive of the 'formative' contributions in the genesis of Marxist thought (bearing in mind, of course, the distinction we have heuristically drawn between 'conception', 'gestation' and 'formation'). Without doubt, Feuerbach is a towering figure on the modern intellectual scene, a gifted and electrifying writer whose impact is still noticeable in many wide areas of learning (paradoxically, this most resolute critic of Christianity receives nowadays the closest attention in university theology departments!). By no means, in other words, is he just the first 'teacher' of Marx. I don't mean, obviously, that Feuerbach is above telling criticism: the very contrary is the case. But here we are mainly interested in his so-called 'transformational critique' of religion and philosophy, central to his thought, and so effectively adapted by Marx in his early writings. Feuerbach himself works out this critique from a position of thoroughgoing *materialism* or perhaps more accurately 'naturalism'. Philosophy must start with its own antithesis, with that which philosophy, thinking, speculating, is definitely *not*. This is 'nature', the world of space, time, matter, the only basic 'reality'. Thinking comes out of nature, and not (as, according to Feuerbach, with Hegel) the other way round. Human beings, too, are 'natural' first of all and essentially: their senses, their appetites, emotions come first, their abstract thinking comes afterwards, and occasioned by the former. (Sometimes Feuerbach embraces a rather crude kind of materialist determinism, as in his celebrated equation of political attitudes with dietary habits.)

Speculative philosophy in general, and religion in particular (and Christianity most pointedly), issue out of a fundamental error, which is the confounding of the 'subject' with the 'predicate'. There is the real subject: the natural human being who *has* thoughts, ideas which are thus his or her 'predicates'. Idealist philosophers like Hegel, however, mistake these mere predicates for the subject, they start out from these abstractions and 'derive' nature, including the existence and character of human beings, from them. Thus these 'predicates', mere consequences, emanations of nature, come to rule over and oppress human beings: the liberation of humanity must therefore mean first of all liberation from the domination of abstractions, the critique and destruction of their seeming *independence*. Most famous is Feuerbach's 'recovery' of the true meaning of transcendental religion in *The Essence of Christianity* (1841). Christian teaching, Feuerbach argues, is absolutely correct in what it *means* but absolutely wrong in what it *says*. It erects the 'predicate' as the 'subject'. 'God' in truth is not a 'being' who created the human race. On the contrary, human beings in the relative backwardness of their understanding created God as an abstraction expressing collectively the qualities they value most. People *mean* that reason, justice, love, benevolence, etc. are the highest human qualities, those which, so to speak, deserve the 'divine' label; so they 'reify' (i.e. bestow substantiality on) these qualities and *call* them the essential qualities of a divinity. The truth for

Feuerbach is that the only kind of 'divinity' is one which resides in actual human *nature*. God is simply a word used to denote the essential nature of humans as 'species-beings', i.e. the qualities that we potentially possess by virtue of being members of the species and that we display individually in a varying measure. *As* 'humans' we are interchangeable, perfectible and thus 'divine'. Religion, through critique, thus leads to the recognition of the human essence; the meaning of theology is anthropology. Feuerbach resolutely denies the tag of 'atheism' – he professes to the perspective of 'anthropotheism', advocating true 'worship', the exaltation of the divinity of human beings, their natural species-qualities, their feelings and thoughts, social relations and institutions.

Feuerbach, consistently with his naturalism, expects the full recovery of humanity from the 'self-estrangement' involved in religion and idealist philosophy in general to occur in *time*, that is, in actual history. He looks, therefore, to the future of the human race which he expects to be glorious and happy, fully rational and at the same time fully communal, with mutual and universal 'love' (*the* highest human-divine quality) dominating all social relations and defining the essence of institutions and activities, e.g. eating, drinking, procreating, as divine pursuits. He actually calls himself a 'communist', on this rarefied level of sentiments and emotions, seeing the essence of humanity in the 'I–thou' relationship. But Feuerbach, although he looks to history for the redemption of mankind, has no real philosophy of history; although a communist, has no communist or revolutionary theory of society or a programme for concrete action; although a naturalist and materialist, does not appreciate the active significance of the very 'material' character of human 'nature', namely the *creative* essence of human labour, production. This last point is made with great force in Marx's *Theses on Feuerbach*. Yet we must note that although Marx turns away from Feuerbach's 'passive' naturalism (and pours scorn on his elevation of 'love'), the Feuerbachian *critical* approach to 'abstractions' like God, pure reason, spirit, philosophy and the like remain a fundamentally *built-in* element in Marxism. Not only does Marx's *Manuscripts*, with its central concept of 'alienated labour', owe almost everything to Feuerbach's inspiration (almost literally oozing in Feuerbachian ter-minology), the approach also essentially defines Marx's mature science of capital. The most conspicuous illustration is of course in the chapter on the 'fetishism of commodities' in the first volume of *Capital*.

There were, obviously, a number of weighty and complicated reasons why Marx (and Engels), having started as enthusiastic adherents, broke with Left Hegelianism. One of these, since it highlights the 'logic' of Left Hegelian thought, should be mentioned here. The situation is rather similar to what we described earlier as the 'logic' of radical democracy pushing it to the espousal of revolutionary communism. Left Hegelian thought set out, as it were, to 'humanize' Hegel's philosophical subject, Spirit, moving from abstractions to palpable entities, from timelessness to concern with an historical future, from speculation to society. The question is: where do you stop? We have just observed the journey undertaken and completed by Feuerbach, for whom the 'real' subject is nature and the human being in nature. But is not the 'human being' also an abstraction, a 'reified' entity similar to God? The momentum of Left Heg-elianism seems to push further along the road of 'hardening' the subject, i.e. the entity which is taken to be ultimately 'real'. The utmost point was probably reached by Max Stirner, that strange and enigmatic figure, with whom Left Hegelianism became almost a *reductio ad absurdum*. Stirner's one big volume, *The Unique One and His Property* (1844), defies classification. Radical and extreme 'Left' in terms of its iconoclastic fervour in destroying all 'abstractions', and in its rather idiosyncratic anarchism, it has also been classed as being among the 'Roots of the Right', by virtue of its hard individualism of a 'possessive' character. Stirner it is who brands Feuerbach as the 'pious atheist' and who mercilessly castigates the latter's notion of an essential human 'species-nature' and the general values derived from it. 'Man' as such, Stirner contends, has no real existence but is just a figment of the philosopher's imagination; revered values and qualities like 'love of our fellows' are – to use a later expression – sublimated forms of mundane psychological states, like fear. Stirner's is a very *cold* look indeed, in sharp contrast to Feuerbach's heated effervescence – and yet the two travel along the same road! Stirner's only hard reality is the 'ego', the 'individual' or the 'unique one': I am my own 'cause', my own end, my own value, and perish humanity. He calls, in authentic Left Hegelian style, for 'liberation' from the muck of a thousand years of 'idealism' and from the superstition of religion (including the materialist religion of humanity). This manifesto of the 'self-conscious egoist' exhibits a final descent from radicalism to nihilism; Stirner's road leads resolutely away from Marx and in the direction – *mutatis mutandis* – of Schopenhauer, Kierkegaard and Nietzsche.

And precisely for the same reason Stirner is a *problem*, or if you like a stumbling-block, in the formation of Marxist thought. It is not for nothing, as historians have rightly suggested, that Marx and Engels thought it necessary to devote by far the longest (and, incidentally, least readable) section of *The German Ideology* to the ridiculing and refutation of 'Saint Max', in excess of the pages employed in a critique of Feuerbach and of 'true socialism'. Whether or not this 'refutation' is successful is largely a matter of judgement; I, for one, do not find it very convincing, not least on account of its diffuseness and stridently *ad hominem* character. But it is not difficult to appreciate Marx's concern, since Marx at this stage basically still subscribed to a form of Left Hegelian humanism *à la* Feuerbach. It is probably true that Marx's and Engels' move from radical humanism to the 'materialist conception of history' (set out for the first time in *The German Ideology*) is *forced* by Stirner's critique of Feuerbach. Whether this shift is a 'sideways movement' of Marx's developing thought or a decisive 'epistemological break', certainly the change is striking – there is a yawning gap between the *language* of Marx's *Manuscripts* and that of *The German Ideology*, and yet barely a year separates the composition of these two texts. This move also signifies – nay, it *expresses* – Marx's fast-intensifying embrace of revolutionary communism and radical political economy, as we have remarked before. On my reading of Marx – again, as has already been mentioned in passing and as it will be argued at greater length in the concluding lecture – the *Manuscripts* is the central text in the story of the genesis of Marxism; it stands, if you like, for the *birth* of Marxism. I am inclined, therefore, to look upon the aforementioned change as *not much more* than a change in language, a mark of 'growth' rather than a turning-point. But this is not the place to enter into an extensive discussion of this complex and rather controversial topic.

The point I would like to make – and this will serve as our conclusion on Left Hegelianism – is that the Marxist critique of Stirner is in fact anticipated by the incisive attack on 'egoism' found in the writings of Moses Hess, Marx's contemporary, admirer, and one-time close collaborator. Hess provides the *positive* link between Left Hegelian humanism and 'French' communism. He is Marx's most *immediate* predecessor, the thinker whose arguments and formulations in the early 1840s are *almost* indistinguishable from the contemporaneous jottings of Marx, with special reference to the latter's *Manuscripts*. Although associated with German 'true socialism', Hess was spared the venomous criticism levelled by Marx and Engels at other representatives of this 'utopian' tendency. Hess set out to achieve the progressive 'synthesis' of German, French and English radicalism before Marx, as his arguments show in *The European Triarchy*. His *Philosophy of the Act* is perhaps the best illustration of the futuristic and practice-oriented winding up of Left Hegelian thought, and his *Essay on Money* for the first time (as acknowledged by Marx himself) applies the Left Hegelian philosophical concept of 'estrangement' directly to political economy and the actual conditions of capitalist society. The Marxist 'take-off' directly follows from these departures. And Hess's critique of Stirner, in the important essay 'The Recent Philosophers', is what (we might say) the Marxist critique *should* have been: clear, pointed, conclusive. Stirner's 'egoist', as Hess points out, is no less an empty abstraction than Feuerbach's 'man', and besides it projects merely a *negative* image of human beings, dependent and vegetative consumers, the playthings of prevailing forces in society, In the advocacy of egoism Stirner merely asserts existing society, the *animal* world of commerce, competition and general exploitation. In as much as human beings have the capacity of truly acting – being creative and having positive sentiments – they must, and will, transcend this world and move towards the establishment of socialism. As Hess puts it, in a statement which is simultaneously the definitive

conclusion of Left Hegelian progress and the conceptual starting-point of Marxism:

> What a philosophical fraud and a bit of modern state
> sagacity it is when the generic-human can only exist in a
> society in which all men self-seekingly cultivate and posit
> themselves. This contradiction will only be solved by
> socialism. It takes the termination and negation of
> philosophy seriously, it will set aside philosophy as well
> as the state, and will write no philosophical books over
> the negation of philosophy, for socialism does not merely
> assert this or that, but it will tell how to deny philosophy
> as mere teaching, and how to finish it off in social life.

We have thus come full circle. The same socialist or communist
goal, which to the 'French' came as the result of following the
path of radical equality and revolution, and to the 'English' via
concentrating on labour in modern society, makes its appearance
for the 'Germans' through the positive negation and transcendence of religion and philosophy. This Germanic, Left Hegelian conclusion (absorbing the other strands) became not only
Marx's immediate departure but remained – as we have
remarked earlier – a component of Marxism as its deepest *moral
base*. Left Hegelian 'humanism' is therefore just as important
for the overall *meaning* of Marxism as the doctrine of class
conflict in history and the scientific analysis of capital and
labour. The humanistic momentum it is which, at the end,
renders Marx's thought more decisively *revolutionary* than the
seemingly harder, more strident doctrines of merely 'political'
or even 'social' revolution; it is this humanism which teaches
Marx that the very *being* of the human species is movement,
progress, revolution, the 'reconquest' of divinity. Without this
'philosophical' revolutionary major premise, the waging of the
class struggle and the critique of capital would ultimately have
little *point*. But then once again, through the revolutionary
premise supplied by Left Hegelian humanism we return visibly
to the *mainstream*, to the original and epoch-making Hegelian
view that 'substance is subject', that the existing world *itself*
moves, that *its* innnermost being is revolutionary. The formation

of Marxist thought thus illuminates for us its gestation, which in turn leads us back to its conception, the triumphant merging in modern times of the idealistic perspective of transcendence with the realistic perspective of understanding.

*   *   *

It would seem appropriate though to wind up this sketch of the formation of Marxism with the raising of some pertinent questions, with reference mainly to the success – or otherwise – of the Marxist 'synthesis'. The foregoing pages should have indicated adequately not just the importance of early socialism (in all its varieties) 'for' Marxism but the value and interest of these departures in themselves. The more we appreciate the true weight of revolutionary communism, utopian socialism and radical humanism in the modern world which witnessed the formation of Marx's thought, the more of course we are inclined to pay tribute to Marx's *achievement* in effecting their synthetic unity. In the lecture to follow I shall attempt to sketch in the more important contours of Marx's own personal development or the first 'fruition' of Marxism. There I shall in the main be preoccupied with the early Marxist texts themselves, and thus no longer explicitly with the elements that went into its formation. Here, therefore, we should venture to *project* forward somewhat and make a comment or two concerning the further-flung fortunes of 'Marxism in the world' – well past its genesis – in the context of those very departures which Marx is supposed to have united and transcended in the first place. What I would like tentatively to suggest is that although Marx's synthesis is without doubt a stupendous achievement, it is not to be seen as total 'victory'. Marxism is and remains *heterogeneous*, and at least some of its basic ambiguities and inadequacies can I believe be understood better if we refer back to its formative elements, chunks which, it seems to me, were not – and perhaps could not have been – completely 'digested' in the thought of the founder.

Marxism, the doctrine and the movement, could it seems to me be profitably analysed in terms of its three basic centrifugal tendencies (which more or less cut across actual 'party' boundaries) of revolutionary militancy, organizational efficiency, and radical criticism – all these are Marxist *values* and at the same time *strategic* concepts. Connoting respectively the values of egalitarian purity and virtue, happiness as the result of max-imized production, and the freedom and superiority of human reason, it requires no great interpretive ingenuity (or audacity) to connect these tendencies up with revolutionary communism, utopian socialism and radical humanism in Marx's formative background, as just surveyed. Now I think two things here are worth noting briefly. In the first place, these tendencies, and the tension between them, are demonstrably present in the tortuous secular development of Marxism in the world. There has been a three-way pull *within* Marxism, fertile and exciting but at the same time causing considerable problems. These problems can be detected in academic texts inspired by and seeking to develop Marxist doctrine, in oppositional movements (of varying inten-sity) seeking power to combat the capitalist order, but most importantly in the evolving nature of Marxist *regimes*, i.e. the problems of Marxism in power. Here, you might say, the official 'dominant melody' of revolutionary puritanism – the Leninist, Trotskyist, Maoist visions, the perspective of Che Guevara, etc. – has had continually to suffer the jarring contrapuntal dis-turbances coming from the mundane desire of people to find happiness *now*, to seek immediate accommodation with the existing world, making *it* more satisfactory from the individual point of view, rather than endeavouring to transcend it alto-gether. The *compromise* (and that's what it is, no mistake) with the bourgeois spirit in latter-day 'market socialism' goes visibly against the grain of revolutionary egalitarianism and virtue. Whether this latter is present only *residually* in official Marxist pronouncements (as an 'ideology' lingering on long after its justifying social 'reality' has passed away) or will reassert itself once again as the living and valid 'core' of Marxism, nobody can tell. But note that this acute political tension – between virtue and happiness, equality and productive efficiency – has also been compounded by the intellectual tension between insti-tutionalized orthodoxies and the free, unruly, subversive 'critical consciousness' of individual Marxist thinkers, devoted to what they see as the true *spirit* of Marxism, its living conscience as opposed to its ossification, whether the 'totalitarian' excesses of revolutionary militancy or the worldliness of 'creeping capitalism' is the target. In Marxism the goals and strategies of equality, happiness and freedom thus continue to collide.

In the second place, one could here observe also the tensions and problems, as it were, occurring *around* Marxism, in the larger arena of radical movements making their presence felt in our modern political and intellectual world. The basic and crucial fact to note – and this would be an embarrassingly naive, childish, pedestrian observation to make, were it not for the overall context – is that Marxism has never succeeded in 'taking over' the entire Left, in mustering the forces of radicalism, socialism, revolution under its 'synthetic' banner. Why? Again, to me it would not appear to be an obviously wrong way to seek an answer – or at least an approximation to an adequate answer – if one were to conjure up the *troubled* character of Marx's original synthesis. Ideas and movements which should have disappeared a long time ago, absorbed into Marxist science, Marxist politics, Marxist social construction, continue to flourish alongside Marxism, on its flanks, among its pores, breathing the same air. Social democrats and moderate 'democratic socialists' (the difference is unimportant right here) take their cue ultimately from Owen and Saint-Simon; militant terrorists, the advocates of the 'cleansing' function of revolutionary violence, are directly in the tradition of Babeuf and Blanqui; sexual radicals of all kinds are resurrecting the basic teaching of Fourier; antinomian rebels, anarchists, dissidents, 'opters-out', carry on more or less the legacy of the critical spirit of Left Hegelian humanism. Has 'Marx' really made that much of a stir? Did 'Marx' (not the individual, of course, but the *figure*) really exist? – one might be beginning to wonder. But we shall return to this topic at the very end of our discussion of the genesis of Marxism, in the concluding section of the fourth lecture.

FRUITION

What comes to fruition in Marx's thought, as a product of intellectual synthesis, is revolutionary communism, the political economy of labour, and humanist philosophy; these represent the utmost (in pure logical terms) development of the political, social and philosophical ideas of modern European liberalism; and liberalism itself is to be seen as the synthetic expression of the two ancient and original perspectives of Western culture, religious idealism and scientific materialism, or the traditions of 'transcendence' and 'understanding', as we have called them here. Marxism both reflects and expresses in its own distinctive idiom the complex nature of its genesis: on one level it is the fusion of an idealistic 'vision' and a materialistic 'insight', on another level it embodies a doctrine of human liberation in the three dimensions of society, nature and the human mind. Such is the overall argument of these four lectures.

It will of course have been noted that in the two previous lectures the three 'ideas' of liberalism and the three radical departures of communism, utopian socialism and radical humanism were discussed in a corresponding particular sequence, politics coming first, society second, and the 'spirit' third. The point has to be made now that – as far as these lectures are concerned – this sequence itself is indifferent or at most warranted only for, as it were, the elegance of presentation. In a pleasingly superficial way only could it be said that politics 'had led to' society and so on. Properly speaking there is no way in which one area can be pronounced 'superior' to any other or that one kind of endeavour – let's say the philosophical 'recognition' of the interdependence of society and state – is necessarily the 'conclusion' of other endeavours. The three dimensions, departures, in truth 'hang' (or 'fall') together, they are complementary, mutually reinforcing, they form – if this is the right term – a kind of symbiotic unity. Their temporally differential 'peaking' in the periods discussed is due to historical accident, nothing more. I felt obliged to make this point mainly for two reasons. Firstly, in Marxist doctrine itself – what we shall later refer to as Marx's 'message' – there is a fairly definite and explicit argument as to which dimension is superior, ultimately 'real', and which is not. Accepting that argument would mean implicitly endorsing the essential validity of Marxism as a whole, and, as has been made clear earlier, this is not the position taken in these lectures. Our verdict on Marxism – in the closing section of this lecture – will be what might be termed a 'discerning' one.

The second reason connects us up with a very intriguing question indeed. What is the significance *for* Marxism that Marx's own intellectual development occurred in a *particular* way, involving a particular 'sequence' of influences, successive reception of ideas, rather than in other ways, other sequences? It is a curious but incontrovertible fact – as conclusively documented as anything can be in the history of ideas – that Marx's own personal development is different from – if not the direct reverse of – the historical 'peaking' of the three ideas, three departures discussed in the foregoing. Marx's career as a whole shows a definite path leading *from* philosophy *through* politics *to* the science of political economy. Marx first appears on the scene, so to speak, as a humanist radical, in essentials a follower of Left Hegelian philosophy; he then becomes a revolutionary communist, with the accent both on 'communism' and on 'revolution' (i.e. displaying the immediate and *practical* direction in which he develops radical humanism); and the undoubted culmination, crowning of Marx's career is as a social scientist, the inventor and advocate of a distinctive theory of the 'laws' of motion of the capitalist economy. Now (unless we unquestionably accept the *Marxist* view itself as to the inherent 'logic' of this sequence) this development certainly appears to be no more than a series of pure historical accidents, viewed on one level. It is an accident that Marx was born into a Lutheran middle-class family of Jewish descent in Trier, and was not the son of an Irish cotton-mill worker in Rochdale; it is an accident also that he attended university in Berlin and Bonn, instead of

Paris and Bordeaux. It had to do with personal and political circumstances, and not with any intellectual reasons, that Marx moved from his native Prussia to exile in France and Belgium, and finally settled in London – his changing domicile, of course, broadly corresponds to the successive predominance of 'German', then 'French', and lastly 'English' ideas in his thought. And we are not moving very far from the category of the 'accidental' (unless, again, inadvertently we are sliding towards the Marxist view itself) either, when we refer to the 'secular' events of mid-nineteenth century European history, i.e. reaction and censorship in Prussia in the 1840s, the surge and then failure of the revolutions of 1848–9, the consolidation of the Bonapartist regime, growing working-class organization in Britain, etc., as being 'influential' in Marx's development.

Nonetheless, it seems to me sensible to assign *some* importance to this – be it 'accidentally' determined – sequence of developmental stages for the *character* of Marxist doctrine, and in particular for its character as 'synthesis' – which, I have been arguing of course, is *the* essential distinguishing mark of this character. To put it somewhat crudely, it is highly unlikely – if not inconceivable – that the Marxist 'synthesis' would have seen the light of day in any other kind of developmental sequence but this. If it had been an O'Marx in Rochdale, or a De Marx in Pau, there would be assuredly no such thing today as Marxism, doctrine or movement. There would have been (given, maybe, an identical genetical structure and even basic family upbringing) *pure* revolutionary communism or *simple* radical political economy. There is no way 'back' to Hegel from Methodism or Owen or Hodgskin, *or* from Jacobinism or Babeuf or Saint-Simon – see, incidentally, the utter contempt with which Marx dismisses Proudhon's 'French' understanding of the Hegelian dialectic in *The Poverty of Philosophy*. We may suggest – without wanting to go too deeply into this and without being necessarily committed to what became the Marxist point of view – that the 'Germanic' philosophical perspective forming Marx's first distinct intellectual departure lent itself particularly easily to expansion into other realms and, in a manner of speaking, to its own supersession. Hegelianism and especially its radical offshoot, as our brief survey in the foregoing lecture should have shown, provide height from which to descend as well as depth from which to rise to a shallower surface; Hegelian philosophy has an *encompassing* nature and simultaneously an open-endedness, or lack of a *hard core*, which renders it inspirational without being dictatorial. It has a quality of 'hot air', of a mind-expanding drug which heightens experience without being itself a particular experience. It could be – and was – 'filled' with content at Marx's hands who thus was able to 'transcend' Hegel, Feuerbach and the rest of them. But of course by the same token Marxism must be recognized for what it carries with it: the same encompassing quality, the same heady air of inspiration. It is this which renders Marxist revolutionary communism something more than pure communism, and Marxist political economy something more than simple political economy.

Concerned as we are here with the genesis of Marxism, in this last lecture we shall concentrate mainly on the 'birth' of this doctrine – or, to resort for the last time to the obstetric imagery which has been employed as the framework of our discussion, the actual and visible 'fruit' that was conceived, nurtured and formed in the various perspectives, ideas and departures mentioned before. The subsequent 'growth' of Marxism will receive only fleeting comment later on. The birth of Marxism will be identified here as the text called posthumously Marx's *Paris Manuscripts* or (more suggestively as to its contents) *Economic-Philosophic Manuscripts*. This implies, obviously, a fairly definite interpretation of Marxism on our part, one moreover which is by no means universally accepted in the world of Marx-scholarship (not to mention the world of 'living' Marxism) – though it is not universally scorned either.

Perhaps I should repeat that I claim no originality whatever for any substantive point made in these lectures. It certainly does seem to me reasonable to adopt this particular interpretive stance, however, and as we go on I shall endeavour to adduce some arguments in its favour (which of course may not *exactly* match those found in similar exegetical exercises). For the moment let me just establish that the interpretation in question negates *eo ipso* a customary, but questionable, categorization of Marx into 'young' and 'mature', or 'humanist' and 'scientific' – in so far as this classification places the *Manuscripts* in the *first* category. Contrary to this, the brunt of the argument advanced in these pages is that the *Manuscripts* is the first properly 'mature' text of Marxism, the stage at which for the first time we can glimpse a distinct Marxist *viewpoint*, a conceptual anchorage which is both 'humanist' and 'scientific'. By 'viewpoint' I mean here a principle of explanation, i.e. Marx's invention of a science of revolutionary political economy out of the various strands, ideas, traditions discussed earlier. Note that the coupling of 'science' and 'revolution' – a paradox at best, a contradiction at worst – is itself a dramatic epitomization of the synthetic character of Marx's work. My argument, perhaps I should add, rests also squarely on the assumption that what is most important and interesting about Marx is what he says concerning the *existing world*, the reason why it persists, and the way it is changing, rather than his desire and intention to change it. Communist 'feelings' would not lift Marx up above the Babeufs, Brays, Feuerbachs; it is his communist *ideas* that do this.

Our substantive treatment of the genesis of Marxism, the story of its birth, will thus conclude with the *Manuscripts*. It will therefore be of more than marginal interest to devote some attention to the path leading up to the writing of this central text of Marxism. There is, indeed, such a phenomenon as the 'young Marx', or 'Marx before Marxism', but this tag should, I think, be properly applied to Marx's output prior to 1844. This relatively short period – consider, Marx was around twenty-six years of age only at the time of the composition of the *Manuscripts* – itself contains a plethora of extremely interesting material, to be sure. It is of course difficult as well as somewhat nebulous to have to select from such literary wealth. But it is also unavoidable. What, then, in the light of our overall perspective in these lectures, I propose to do is to highlight just those aspects of Marx's early intellectual maturation which seem directly to point towards the formulation of the Marxist viewpoint in the *Manuscripts*. Accordingly, I shall devote a brief section first to the period up to 1842, i.e. Marx's so-called 'radical democratic' phase. Here as we shall see Marx is still heavily imbued with *politics* and *philosophy*. The second period, from 1842 to 1844, is 'transitional' in that it witnesses Marx's decisive movement away from both philosophy and politics, and his emerging substantive focus on *society*. Albeit in this sense 'negative', the interest and importance of this period is by no means to be belittled: it is now that Marx composes some of his most incisive *critiques*, containing perhaps the best – most readable – pieces in his total output, from a 'belletristic' point of view at any rate. And then finally we shall confront the *Manuscripts*, signifying Marx's explicit embracing of communism and – what is even more noteworthy – his 'hardening' of the concept of society into the concept of 'alienated labour', thus reaching his distinctive viewpoint. In an interesting way, it might be said, this process of development towards the Marxist viewpoint itself reproduces on a miniature scale the long and tortuous story of its genesis in the Western tradition – there is a parallel, in other words, between the 'phylogenesis' and 'ontogenesis' of Marxism. Let's just say that this parallel is quite remarkable, though probably without any deeper significance. Still, it *is* true that Marx's own personal development also has an 'idealistic' and 'moral' foundation, and goes through the phases of 'liberal' rationalism, radical democracy, a 'social critique' reminiscent of utopianism, and finally the 'soaring thought' of humanist philosophy.

*   *   *

Marx's earnest belief in morality and formal adherence to revealed religion (Lutheran Christianity) can be glimpsed from a piece of school writing, dated 1835, reprinted in his *Collected Works*. The piece, entitled 'Reflections of a Young Man on the Choice of a Profession', enunciates Marx's view that the highest calling of the individual is to serve the interests of humanity and to perfect oneself – this being, as Marx writes, also the teaching of 'our religion'. But by the time he is a student of law at the Royal Prussian University of Berlin, Marx is already a firm adherent of modern philosophy, which now supplies the basis of his moral beliefs. Absorbed in Kant and Fichte, he finds Hegel at first a 'craggy melody', in a well-known passage from a letter to his father in 1837. Apparently it was due to a drawn-out period of illness in Berlin that Marx came thoroughly to digest the Hegelian texts – another historical accident. He was, at this time, meeting regularly with disciples of Hegel, the more radical-minded of whom were exerting an increasing influence on him. Marx's doctoral thesis, set on the atomic theories of Democritus and Epicurus, was prepared under the supervision of the eminent Left Hegelian philosopher and theologian, Bruno Bauer, who was then *Dozent* at the University of Bonn. It is in the Preface to the thesis, written in 1841, that Marx for the first time formulates an explicit *humanist* viewpoint, directly in line with Left Hegelian thought. Declaring Prometheus to be the epitome of humanity – the mythical figure who hated all gods and endeavoured to rise against them – Marx states his conviction that there is no divinity anywhere higher than human self-consciousness. It is this apotheosis of 'self-consciousness', a hallmark especially of Bauer's Left Hegelian philosophy, which only a couple of years or so later Marx will ridicule with such venom in *The Holy Family*. But it is an integral part of his own original perspective, too. Marx, so we are told, was at this time contemplating taking up an academic career in Bonn, under Bauer's patronage. But Bauer was dismissed from his position in 1841, following a conservative – and anti-Hegelian – turn in the educational policies of the Prussian government. Yet another historical accident, if you like (and the mind boggles at the thought of Marx settling down as a 'Professor' in a German university), resulting in Marx's leaving the world of academe for good and taking up full-time radical journalism. This, as it were, remained Marx's lifetime occupation and an important source of his income.

Marx first made a name for himself as the editor of the radical (though not socialist) *Rheinische Zeitung*. Of his numerous incisive articles and editorials from this period, two will deserve attention here. The piece, entitled 'The Leading Article of No. 179 of the *Kölnische Zeitung*' (July 1842), reveals Marx's attachment to philosophy as well as his faith in the modern state. It is, in tone and many other ways, an unmistakably 'Hegelian' article. For Marx, philosophy at this time appears as the only way to the reaching of truth, 'universal' truth about reality and about the 'universal' character of the human species. The search for truth, 'scientific' endeavour, is the highest calling for man, undertaken and carried on for its own sake; it is not to be subservient to any other authority, like custom or religion. Marx's argument is to be seen in the context of the burning issue of governmental censorship, then raging. Marx here also declares the state to be 'moral association', with its own gravity and independence. The state is not the 'Christian' state but the universal expression of the free human spirit. Like philosophy, the state is the embodiment of human freedom and universality. In a tone which is strongly reminiscent of Hegelian texts, Marx calls upon the state to educate its members, to fulfil its task by 'converting the aims of the individual into general aims, crude instinct into moral inclination, natural independence into spiritual freedom'. It will be recalled that in our lecture on the 'gestation' of Marxism above special emphasis was placed on Hegel's concept of the state, pointing both backwards and forwards, with a connection to Marxist 'communism'. This then – Marx's early notion of the state as moral and educative association – can be seen as the first stage in this forward development. Again, pointedly, Marx refers in this article to the succession of the giants of European political philosophy, to Machiavelli, Hobbes, Spinoza, Grotius, Rousseau, Fichte and Hegel, who according to Marx all tended to define the state in this way. At this point – though probably not later on – Marx does see himself as being in the *mainstream* of European thought, as a direct successor to the philosophers mentioned. Marx's perspective, that is to say, is now the very same *freedom of reason* characterizing the 'soaring thought' of liberalism and the various radical departures issuing therefrom.

However, the next and important point to note is that even at this early philosophical, moralistic and 'statist' stage of his development, Marx in his writings provides definite glimpses of what is to become his mature standpoint. Marx does, as it were, ask himself the question (in a way which would not have been congenial to his Left Hegelian mentors) as to why the 'freedom of reason' does *not* obtain in actual human life and government and social relations? Why is it that only the 'spirit' is free? He is led on, in searching for an adequate answer, to observing social *division* and *conflict* and declaring these to be the chief obstacles to the realization of freedom in the modern state – note that for him it is not ignorance and superstition, or a matter chiefly to do with 'consciousness' (as it was, in the main, for the likes of Bauer and Feuerbach as well as the utopian socialists). This expressly political and if you like 'sociological' interest of the young Marx, coming to *infuse* (though not for some time to 'supersede') his radical humanist philosophy, comes out most dramatically in the famous article in the *Rheinische Zeitung* on 'Debates on the Law on Thefts of Wood' (October 1842). The context here was a current conservative proposal to alter the law, making the gathering of fallen wood in the forests a criminal offence. The gathering of wood had up to then apparently been allowed, a kind of customary right of the poor villagers. Marx argues vehemently against this proposed new legislation, and in the course of his argument he makes what I think are two general points, both of far-reaching significance in view of the fully-fledged doctrine of Marxism later.

The first point concerns the poor themselves who, as Marx says, have had this elemental right to 'nature' in the past. The poor possessed this right, in the first place, by virtue of being *like* 'nature' themselves, an indistinguishable part of nature, like the fallen twigs. The poor were those who owned nothing but themselves. But in the second place the poor made the wood *theirs* by right, through the very activity of gathering. The poor thus – representing, as it were, the human species in nature – were introducing 'order' into nature, stamping the right of humanity on to nature. It is not difficult – and certainly not sensational – to note in this argument a distant echo of liberalism, with pointed reference to Locke's dictum on human 'labour' creating the natural right to property, and to Hegel's very firm and explicit stand on the absolute right of 'Spirit' against nature. However, what I think is a lot more interesting here is to note an, as it were, *forward-pointing* 'echo', projecting the distinctive Marxist perspective fully worked out some years later. The *continuity* of the modern European mainstream and Marxism is indeed dramatically demonstrated here. Marx, as far as I am aware, had no knowledge at this time of 'English' political economy and knew nothing, in particular, about the Ricardian socialists. Yet at this point we can already detect a groping formulation of what is to become eventually Marx's *labour theory of value*. The concept – or 'pre-concept', if we want to be pedantic – thus comes to Marx not from science but from humanist philosophy infused with social criticism. The poor are those who 'own nothing but themselves' – this is also the essential core of the Marxist definition of the 'wage-earner' in capitalist society later. And for Marx it is the poor – by virtue of *being* poor, like 'fallen twigs' – who create right (i.e. 'value') by virtue of their sheer *activity*. A fundamental element in the build-up of Marx's revolutionary science of political economy – the proposition, namely, that in human society *labour*, productive activity, is what counts, and nothing else does – is therefore already present in 1842, even *before* Marx becomes a 'revolutionary' and a 'communist'.

But it seems to me that we can go even further than this. Marx in the same article pointedly observes the elemental conflict between the 'private interest' of the forest owners and the general moral interest supposedly represented by the state. The state *should* represent also the interests of those who own nothing but themselves – but in fact it does not. The state is thus reduced to subservience, it is no longer true to its own essential moral nature, in practice it only serves the interests of the owners. Now on one level we can certainly detect here a groping move towards the radical denunciation of private property, which is of couse a cornerstone of Marx's doctrine later on. In actual fact, Marx does not at this point attack private property as such. He does something much more interesting. To wit, he glimpses a fundamental conflict of interest lurking *behind* the clash of interest of owners and the gatherers of wood. What on the more immediate level appears as the interest of the forest owners turns out to be not *their* interest at all. It is the 'interest' of the *wood* – that is to say, the interest of nature thus pitted clandestinely against the interest of humanity. 'Private' interest, in other words, is not 'human' interest in the proper sense. Humans are here sacrificed to nature, to the wood. Just as the state is subservient to the owners, the latter in turn are in thrall to the 'wooden idol' which they merely represent and which hence dominates society through them. As Marx writes:

> Cruelty is a characteristic feature of laws dictated by
> cowardice, for cowardice can be energetic only by being

cruel. Private interest, however, is always cowardly, for its heart, its soul, is an external object, which can always be wrenched away and injured, and who has not trembled at the danger of losing heart and soul? How could the selfish legislator be human when something inhuman, an alien material essence, is his supreme essence?

If this statement – in the medium of rhetorical, moralizing journalism, soon to be discarded – does not encapsulate the fermenting but *continuous* 'essence' of Marxist doctrine, then I don't know what does. This essence, I would argue, has precisely to do with the sharp contrasting of the 'human essence' to an 'alien material essence'. The former clearly stands for spirit, reason, freedom, morality. The latter though – the 'wooden idol' masquerading as 'private interest' – actually *rules* over humanity, exerts its cruel domination, enslaves the spirit, turns reason into irrationality. Here we have then the first clear intimation of the direction of Marx's thought towards the formulation of the concept of alienated labour in the *Manuscripts*. From there, of course, the next step is the formulation of the concept of *capital* by Marx. Thus in this 1842 article *both* prongs of Marxist revolutionary political economy already signify their presence, though only embryonically or as 'raindrops' heralding a heavy storm: on the one hand there is 'labour' as spirit, as sheer activity, as humanity, and on the other hand there is 'capital' as idol-worship, as estranged labour, as private property and interest, as – in the last resort – *nature* posing a dire threat to the human race.

It is of interest and relevance to note here, furthermore, that at the time of composing these two – what could be called – key articles as editor of the *Rheinische Zeitung*, Marx still does not profess himself to be a 'communist'. On the contrary, he displays an attitude to communism – seen as a doctrine imported from France – which is not too short of being dismissive; at best it comes forth as a rather 'cool' view of communism. There is, I think, a fairly important general point to be made in this connection. Marx's road to communism, it seems to me, is quite different from that travelled by many (or perhaps most) of his contemporaries, not to mention his spiritual descendants and generations of disciples. With the latter, so often, there is a pure, glowing, transcendent, heavenly *vision*, the 'good society' of freedom, peace, brotherhood, happiness. In other words, the *whole* comes first, or an emotional attachment to a world which is epitomized in the term, 'communism', itself. Adherents are *then* educated into the details, the nitty-gritty of communist mentality, political strategy, the practical tasks of communist construction. Thus even if they get disillusioned by the mundane reality of communism – as so frequently they do – they still find it hard, if not impossible, to relinquish the original dream, the ideal, the vision, the 'whole' which attracted them in the first place. Not so with Marx. As I endeavoured to show in the preceding paragraphs, Marx takes up communism, as it were, by instalments. He is not, initially at any rate, in the least attracted by the pure vision of communism. Instead he has philosophical convictions, i.e. radical humanism, he has moral ideas, i.e. the state as moral association, and he has a critical view of existing society, i.e. of the state's subservience to an 'alien material essence'. It is these separate, though interrelated, bits of argument and moral conviction which later will be seen to *fit* communism, or perhaps one should rather say communism as a general framework will come to fit *them*. Thus, although it would be pointless to deny that Marx, from 1844 onwards, comes to embrace the pure vision of communism also, with him it is a *rational* affair from the very beginning. Communism for Marx is a working analytical *concept* as well as a visionary ideal, a tool of understanding as well as an aim to work for. Perhaps this is one significant reason why Marx – alone among major communist thinkers in the modern age – remains so noticeably reticent when it comes to describing communism as pure vision. And perhaps Marx – though we have, of course, no way of knowing or even guessing, and even if we did 'know' it wouldn't be terribly important – would for the same reason have been readier than his latter-day followers to relinquish or modify the vision when directly confronted by the reality.

* * *

The next phase in Marx's intellectual development (around 1843) is 'transitional' in the precise sense of containing an independent view, building on the values and social criticism of the newspaper articles commented on above, but one which will itself be superseded soon by the perspective of the *Manuscripts*. In fact it is a very interesting phase to study, partly on account of the intrinsic qualities of Marx's arguments and partly because it shows the precise manner of Marx's emancipation from the tutelage of Hegel and the Left Hegelians. There are three import-ant pieces to be considered from this period. Firstly the long, difficult and somewhat arcane manuscript 'Critique of Hegel's *Philosophy of Right*', and then two major articles published in the *Deutsch-Französische Jahrbücher* (of which Marx was then co-editor) in 1844, viz. 'On the Jewish Question' and 'Intro-duction to a Critique of Hegel's *Philosophy of Right*'. The two latter pieces are short, lucid, readable, displaying a quality of freshness and incisiveness often missing from Marx's great 'scientific' works (whose intellectual excellence tends to be marred by their abstruseness and occasionally even dogmatism); the early pieces show us Marx as a gifted stylist, too.

The transition in Marx's thought witnessed in this period can in the first place be usefully characterized in negative terms: Marx is now moving away from philosophy towards 'practical' realization, away from the state towards the very dissolution of the (Hegelian) concept of the state, and away from society towards radical social criticism. Yet this is still not to be seen as a *very* sharp break with ideas expressed by Marx earlier – there *are* no sharp breaks in the history of political thought, once we study it in close enough detail – and continuity here at any rate is easily shown on the level of deeply held values. In particular, and as we have suggested before, Marx's uncom-promising dismissal of the Hegelian state as an organizing concept (denoting a specific institutional structure) does not necessarily mean his corresponding rejection of it as *moral* concept or underlying moral quality. On the contrary, it would seem sensible to argue that Marx's emerging vision and under-standing of communism as the unity of the individual and the species actually build on, and merely verbally redefine, his own original Hegelian view of the state as 'true moral association'. These considerations might then lead to a characterization of the transition in Marx's thought in positive terms: it is at this time that Marx places the Feuerbachian concept of the human 'species-being' into the centre of his perspective, that he formulates a notion of 'human emancipation' defined in sharp contrast to merely 'political' liberation, and finally that he comes to discover in the 'proletariat' the locus, agent and symbolic expression of human emancipation. Note that all these three departures will in turn be superseded – though by no means totally abandoned – in the *Manuscripts*.

Marx's 'Critique of Hegel's *Philosophy of Right*', unpublished until the twentieth century, contains about 120 pages of detailed, analytical commentary on a section (Parts 261–313) of this weighty and important Hegelian text. Apparently it was composed during Marx's honeymoon in Kreuznach in 1843; it is obviously incomplete, with parts of the manuscript missing. The content of the 'Critique' can conveniently be treated under three headings (intermixed in the text itself). As we have said, it is no easy reading. In the first place, it contains a criticism of Hegel's philosophical method and general principles of philosophy. There are in fact only a couple of pithy paragraphs on the latter topic, which is unfortunate, since Marx rarely got into the habit later on of addressing himself to general philosophical questions *per se*. Marx's standpoint in this piece clearly derives from Feuerbach. Following his Left Hegelian mentor, Marx charges Hegel here with the 'idealistic' error of transposing 'subject' and 'predicate' in his philosophy of the state. For Hegel the starting-point is the 'idea', not the reality; he derives actual people, the substance of state and society, from such 'abstractions' as *the* state, *the* will, sovereignty. Furthermore Hegel, so Marx argues, is mistaken on the notion of 'contradiction': it is not the case, as Hegel seems to have thought, that contradictory essences themselves constitute the nature of reality or 'Spirit'. There are, for Marx, seeming contradictions of 'existence' within the same essence (like North and South Pole) which pose no serious problems for philosophy, and contradictory 'essences' (like pole and non-pole) which cannot be philosophically brought together. The real problem comes up when contradictions occur between a real substance and its 'abstraction'. He cites the case of religion, here too following closely on Feuerbach's lead. Like the latter, Marx believes and argues that these, as it were, really

142

pernicious contradictions can and should be eliminated. This radical separation of the 'real' and the 'abstraction', based here on Left Hegelian philosophy, will in Marx's case lead directly to the concept of alienation in the *Manuscripts*, the Marxist theory of 'ideology', and the exposure of the 'fetishism of commodities' in *Capital*.

In the second place, Marx engages in a detailed criticism of certain concrete elements found in Hegel's philosophy of the state. Here Marx seems to be on fairly firm ground and his style soars in a string of cutting witticisms. Quite convincingly, I think, he is able to show that Hegel's state – in terms of its concrete institutional parts – is neither rational, nor modern, nor free. It contains archaic elements and is steeped in 'medievalism'. Hegel's extolling of the landed aristocracy merely reflects the domination of property over people – Marx's argument here is noticeably similar to the one already mentioned in the newspaper article on the Wood Theft Laws. Hegel's 'universal class' of civil servants, likewise, shows up the hidden power of a 'particular interest' in the state. But Marx's special venom is poured out on Hegel's notion of hereditary constitutional monarchy – somewhat unnecessarily, it might seem, for this does not seem to be central to the basic Hegelian *idea* of the state as such (although this is, admittedly, an arguable point), and also since Marx in the same piece pours a great deal of scorn likewise on more 'modern' and 'rational' state forms, with special reference to the 'republic'. However, Marx's contemptuous and witty demolition of the hereditary principle – elevating sexual activity to be the highest political activity – does make for enjoyable reading.

In the third and possibly most important instance, in this manuscript Marx advances – for the first and almost the last time (but also found in 'On the Jewish Question') – a string of critical arguments on the 'state' as such, in detail and with considerable force. From extolling the state previously as 'true moral association' he has now in substance moved to a view of pronouncing the state as such – i.e. every form of state – an expression of human *self-estrangement*. Living in the state, under general laws and accepting the role of abstract citizenship, means *eo ipso* being divorced from real life. The 'atomized' individuals ostensibly 'represented' in modern state institutions are in truth people estranged from their proper human selves. The state signifies the imposition of a lifeless and falsifying 'form' on living people who are then said (by Hegel, according to Marx) to be 'constituted' by the state. Constitutions, so Marx argues with vehemence, proceed from real, living individuals, and not the other way around, substance coming very definitely before form – or, as political scientists would probably put it these days, processes are prior to structures. Thus Marx at this point – through dismissing the state as such – leaves behind *on this particular level* the entire modern liberal tradition of 'political' philosophy (and hence, according to some commentators, does not deserve to be treated as a 'political thinker'). Humanity *directly* now – the living substance of individuals expressing their universal species-character – is Marx's 'subject', and all petrified forms are 'predicates'. The seemingly rational, free and modern state form of 'republic', as we have already remarked above, is dismissed by Marx almost in the same breath as the monarchy. To the republic Marx here contrasts 'democracy' which to him is 'the solved riddle of all constitutions', where the constitution itself is revealed as the 'free product of man'.

Marx's notion of democracy here is certainly very intriguing. What can 'democracy' *mean* if it is beyond the state form altogether, beyond politics, beyond representation, beyond any *binding* form of constitution? What meaning does a constitution have if it is literally a 'product', nothing else, and therefore in no sense binding on its makers, the people? In a way, it could be said, Marx here is really pushing the liberal notion of *society* (and let's forget Hegel, as immediate context, for the moment) to its absurd logical limit, viz. the idea of a 'contract', based on the fiction of individuals in their 'natural state' consciously and intentionally setting up laws, government, various institutions. In other words, what Marx at bottom is opposing to Hegel's state is a variant derivation of Adam Smith's 'natural society' – a retrograde step, therefore, in a sense. Projecting forward, again, it could be suggested that this early Marxist notion of democracy is a kind of *halfway house* to Marx's concept of communism in the *Manuscripts*, i.e. communism which is squarely, literally meant to lie beyond politics and the state. But yet again there are certain indications in this manuscript critique that Marx, in spite of his strongly worded denunciation of Hegel's philosophy of the state, is still moving within an Hegelian universe, in a broader and deeper sense. That is, Marx's understanding of 'democracy' is not that far removed from his earlier notion of a 'true moral association' of rational, free, equal individuals whose *political* being is the same as their *social* being. There is, in other words, a reduction of state to society just as much as a reduction of society to state – that is, the *pure* Hegelian idea of the state. (The point made earlier concerning the 'forward-looking' aspect of Hegel's concept of the state should be recalled here.) It is of great interest to note that – very much in the manner of Hegel – Marx seems in the 'Critique' positively to advocate *functional* representation, as contrasted to 'abstract' individual representation, on the state level. This brings state and society visibly and effectively together: the various 'species-activities' represent individuals as they really *are*, in society, and at the same time they all represent the universal species. And again, just as there is a clearly detectable retrospective linkage in Marx's emerging perspective, there is a luminous foreshadowing of the concept of 'abstract labour', as elaborated in the mature Marxist science of political economy.

In the 'Critique', then, Marx reaches the point of exposing the 'insubstantiality' of the abstract political state with the corresponding stress on the substantiality of 'society'. But what, after all, is modern 'society' and *why* should it have created its unreal, 'heavenly' counterpart in the state? The answer to that is supplied in Marx's 'On the Jewish Question', an article written around the same time as the 'Critique'. Undoubtedly the best, most incisive and challenging of Marx's works still recognizably in the genre of 'political philosophy' (although, paradoxically maybe, it reinforces Marx's radically critical, dismissive view of politics), the article also marks his final rejection and transcendence of the 'social' idea of liberalism – with which, as we have noted above, there is some amount of flirting in the 'Critique'. 'On the Jewish Question' for the first time focuses on the *reality* of society, containing Marx's initial and groping – but nonetheless concrete – analysis of it. The context of the article is provided by two pieces by the Left Hegelian writer

Bruno Bauer who, from the point of view of radical liberalism, raises doubts about the feasibility of Jewish emancipation in the 'Christian' German states, and also about Jews being themselves capable of emancipation, as long as they adhere to their own religious culture. Bauer looks to the completely 'secularized' state (like the USA and France) for political emancipation, applicable to individuals who themselves are secularized in their consciousness. This 'left liberal' stance presents Marx with an opportunity to bring forth an exceptionally scathing critique of the liberal perspective as such, going to the very conceptual bottom of it, and grasping in the process the notions of the 'religious' and the 'secular' in one fundamental category. The striking novelty of Marx's view – emerging out of a Left Hegelian humanist background – is not to be underestimated. The conceptual *breakthrough* effected by Marx in 'On the Jewish Question' is without doubt among the most impressive of his intellectual achievements.

Why should Bauer, or anybody for that matter, think that the modern 'secular state' properly emancipates, liberates individuals? – asks Marx. The secular state can only be concerned with 'political' emancipation, which is important in itself (marking progress from absolutism, feudal inequalities, the *ancien régime*, to modernity) but ultimately no more than a stage in the process leading to 'human emancipation'. The modern secular state is only *seemingly* 'atheist', has only seemingly transcended religion; in reality it is the actual embodiment, the direct expression of Christianity. The state represents the Christian 'heaven' where all individuals are supposed to be free, equal and dignified as 'citizens'. It is a world of fantasy, of make-believe. The heaven of the state disguises, obscures the real earth of society. And here comes the crunch: society creates the state as heavenly compensation (as it also spawns organized and dogmatic religion, the 'opium of the people') because *it itself*, society, embodies human life, consciousness and social relations, in an *estranged* form. Society, far from being 'natural', is the expression of a most sordid, most inhuman, most unnatural kind of reality conceivable. To live in a so-called modern 'civil society' (Marx here still habitually uses the Hegelian term) is *eo ipso* degrading for human beings. This society falsifies the real nature of individuals as universal species-beings by confirming them in their narrow, egoistic selves. They are mere *slaves* to their own estranged being, fragmentary shadows of their proper human 'social powers' now running amuck. Marx here contemptuously dismisses the great crowning document of the French Revolution, the 'Declaration of the Rights of Man and Citizen'. What rights? What man? In modern society 'liberty' pertains to *isolated monads*, individuals, in order to preserve their *separation* from their fellows and thereby to hinder their own proper human liberation. What human emancipation requires is freedom *from* religion, not *of* religion, freedom *from* property, not *of* property. It requires, in the final analysis, the overcoming and repossessing of the 'unrestrained movement of material and spiritual elements' in human life and activity. Already here, therefore, we see a prefiguration of Marx's notion of *capital* later, defined as human labour in its estranged form. The freedom of capital, or in terms of the misleading euphemism 'free enterprise', means likewise the continuing slavery of labour; proper human freedom is freedom *from* enterprise.

There is, however, a somewhat surprising and disturbing twist in the closing section of Marx's article, which we may as well mention briefly. If Marx dismisses Christianity with contempt, he now turns to Judaism with real venom and hatred. What nonsense it is to say, as Bruno Bauer does, that the modern world represents the triumph of Christianity over Judaism, as a more 'rational' principle of religion, espousing individual freedom and equality. In truth, Marx asserts, modern society signifies the complete *victory* of Judaism over Christianity. Just as 'society' is the real actor, real substance, of the modern world, and the 'state' is merely its heavenly shadow, reflection, so Judaism is the real substantial principle of society, the guiding perspective of egoistic individuals *in practice*, whereas Christianity is reduced to meaningless Sunday observance. In becoming modern and 'secular', Christians have in fact become 'everyday Jews'. Society is dominated by the Judaic spirit of 'Mammon', the spirit of egoism, personal gain, exchange, commerce; the 'nationality' of the member of civil society is the 'abstract' Judaic identity of the merchant (compare this to the famous statement of the *Communist Manifesto* some years later about capital having broken down national barriers). The ringing coda of Marx's article calls for the liberation of modern society from Judaism as the means to the achievement of human emancipation.

Perhaps we could make a short comment or two on this apparent 'anti-semitic' outburst of Marx's (which, not surprisingly, has created a distinctive exegetical literature of its own). That Marx was not a 'racialist' in any obvious sense is certain, and it is also true that the perspective and analysis of civil society he puts forward in this article are superseded later – though note that 'On the Jewish Question' was actually published in 1844 and Marx never formally repudiated its stance. Again, Marx's and Engels' 'colloquial' anti-semitism, as shown in their correspondence for example, is wholly inconsequential, merely reflecting Central European cultural and class prejudices prevalent at the time. But still two points seem worth making briefly. The first one is rather controversial but so be it. It is simply that – the enormous conceptual chasm between them notwithstanding – Marx's stance here shows at least as it were an 'existential' linkage between the Marxist and the later emerging fascist critiques of *modernity*, with its universal egoism, cosmopolitanism, acquisitiveness, 'abstract' social relations. It is as though the whole prevailing ethos of modern liberalism came in time to be attacked from two opposed angles, and subsequent history provides ample illustration of the truth of the adage that 'the enemy of my enemy is my friend'. But the second – and of couse here much more relevant – point to make is that the *language* of Marx's critical stance should not deceive us as to its deeper *spirit*: while attacking the ethos of Judaism as *petrified*, and of Christianity as *fantastic*, and the world of modern European state and society *in toto* as 'estranged', topsy-turvy, degrading, inhuman, oppressive, self-contradictory, Marx merely wishes to give verbal expression to this world, and these long-standing traditions, as still *moving*. His perspective, therefore, is not alien to the European tradition but merely represents a *transvalued* Judaism, Christianity, and modern liberalism.

The third piece to be considered under the heading, 'transition', is a fiery programmatic article, entitled 'Towards a Critique of Hegel's *Philosophy of Right*. Introduction'. In it, however, we find relatively little attention devoted to the Hegelian text referred to in the title. Instead, the article sets out with rhetorical vehemence the Marxist denunciation of religion (the famous 'opium' statement is made here), in substance merely repeating points made elsewhere, and makes for the first time the equally renowned remarks about the 'backwardness' of Germany in relation to France and Britain. The significance of this article – its theoretical content is rather shallow compared to 'On the Jewish Question' – lies precisely in the graphic and striking manner in which it shows Marx's *way out* of the Germanic cultural universe. Germany, Marx argues, is backward compared to Britain and France in terms of its politics and its society. The latter countries achieved modern political *revolutions*. Germany could not, because its society did not bring forth a rising 'class' which could act as political leader, i.e. an equivalent of the modern 'bourgeoisie'. However, Marx goes on, Germany *is* equal to these West European states and societies in one all-important respect, namely in its 'thought', in its advanced philosophical standpoint – indeed, Marx intimates not at all darkly that he believes German philosophy to be superior to its French and British counterparts. It is in the perspective of German philosphy *only* (Marx of course means Hegelian philosophy in its radical development) that the imminent transcendence by human beings of their present consciousness, life conditions and social relations – their potential *divinity* in recognizing and accepting no higher moral authority over themselves – is decisively set out, formulated as a realizable historical programme.

However, while Marx declares German humanist philosophy to be *highest*, by the same token he recognizes its *emptiness*. Thus the elements of his mighty synthesis – as we remarked briefly at the beginning of this lecture – are seen to be coming together smoothly, naturally, logically; they invite and complement one another. Philosophy bestows the final illumination on politics and society but it is the latter that supply the real basis, real substance of philosophy itself. Philosophy, having achieved its summit in radical humanism, is now completely spent and has to 'descend' to its own ground; there is no further sense in and room for mere 'speculation'; the end of philosophy is its *realization* in political and social practice. It is at this point that Marx focuses his attention on the 'proletariat'. Philosophy is to be realized, the divinity of humanity to be proven, but philosophy is impotent to achieve this task on its own. The proletariat *in Germany* – and this is a significant point – will supply, so Marx argues, the 'material element' necessary to the realization of philosophy. This 'class' does not yet properly exist but has to be 'formed', out of those made artificially poor in modern conditions (a very distant echo here of Hegel's famous 'Police' section in *The Philosophy of Right*). Marx envisages this proletariat as the *negative* image of humanity, the class that is effectively deprived of its humanity and *therefore* becomes the agent of *universal* 'human emancipation'. Again, the ringing metaphors abound: the weapon of criticism is to be supplanted by the criticism of the weapon, philosophy and the proletariat will join in the revolution as respectively its head and its heart. In Germany there is not going to be a political revolution; Germany will represent – will *be*, we might be tempted to say – *human* emancipation in its triumphant climax. Almost all the essential ingredients of Marxism are already here, disjointed and half-formed but nevertheless vibrant, fertile. When all possible allowances are made, then, for the reality and importance of Marx's various *sideways* movements later, into French revolutionary politics and English political economy in particular, could one really say that Marx ever leaves 'German philosophy' behind? Or, that which itself has given rise to German philosophy, the soaring thought of the European Enlightenment? Or Christianity and Judaism and classical philosophy which generated the Enlightenment and modernity? What *would* Marxism be if not their palpable offspring?

The transition period thus ends with Marx already in intellectual possession of such key Marxist concepts as class, the proletariat, social or 'human' emancipation, the critique of ideology, the state and 'atomistic' modern society. We have even detected earlier on a faint embryonic projection of the concepts of abstract labour and the fetishism of commodities. All this comes at this time out of the fertile union of philosophy and politics, with philosophy being definitely the dominant partner – in spite of Marx's absorbing of various accounts of French communism (notably the famous work by Lorenz von Stein), he has yet to make his more intimate acquaintance with the real world of revolution. But what is most conspicuously absent from Marx's thought as yet is political economy *qua* 'science'. When Marx properly and consciously 'receives' – to use the Continental academic term – the teachings of the political economists in the summer of 1844, he has notions himself to *take* to this reception, notions which the new framework will fit snugly. In the *Manuscripts* of 1844 – to which we will now turn in this last substantive section of the four lectures – we find a superior ordering of these febrile notions, and also their hardening or *concretization*. Up to the *Manuscripts*, it might be suggested as a heuristic aid, Marx's ideas show 'condensation' in two areas. His critical thought focuses on 'civil society'. And his constructive – if you like visionary – thought centres on the ideal of 'human emancipation'. It is not in the least an accident that both will be concretized *together*, and *with* Marx's 'reception' of political economy, as clearly demonstrated in the pages of the *Manuscripts*. The critique of civil society issues in the concept of alienated labour, later 'hardened' even further as the concept of capital. And the ideal of human emancipation is simultaneously condensed, triumphantly transfigured in Marx's concept of communism.

* * *

The view that the *Economic-Philosophic Manuscripts of 1844* is the first rough draft of Marx's epoch-making magnum opus, *Capital: a Critique of Political Economy*, is not new but it is still not very popular, let alone generally accepted, in the world of Marx-studies. I will later expend a little bit of effort on endeavouring to make this interpretation more sensible than it might appear at first glance, mainly by highlighting what to me comes forth as the underlying and guiding principle of Marxist science, viz. alienated labour. But the first sally towards that argument must be the modest – though I believe highly relevant – observation that in the *Manuscripts*, Marx's notebooks, by far the most important subject matter is the texts of political economists, notably Smith's *Wealth of Nations*, followed in terms of extent as well as depth by a series of 'social comments' on actual conditions in England; then come chunks of economic history, and 'philosophy' proper is last in the row. Actually only one short section of the *Manuscripts*, dealing with Hegel's *Phenomenology of Spirit*, can be said to have a narrowly 'philosophical' concern, and even this is shot through with economic comment, Marx squarely arguing from his newly discovered Archimedean fulcrum of political economy. At most it could be said that this sequential order of *preoccupations* resembles much more clearly Marx's subsequent works, with special reference to *Capital*, than his writings before. The book *Capital* itself, in broad terms, consists of an overpowering amalgam of scientific argumentation (which can be validly regarded as Marx's critical development of the 'texts' of the political economists), economic history and social observation. But at least it could be said that in the *Manuscripts* Marx displays a novel interest, intellectual curiosity and excitement certainly not shown before, that he becomes (for a short while at any rate) an avid 'student'. It is surely undeniable that Marx is *impressed* by the subject of political economy *qua* science much more than he was ever impressed by philosophy or politics. If ever Marx can be said to turn a new leaf, it is at this point, in the *Manuscripts* where his most pregnant formulations actually grow out of direct comment on passages transcribed at length from political economy texts.

After this preliminary observation, however, the next point to make is that Marx's famous concept of 'alienation' (*Entaüsserung*), used in the *Manuscripts* interchangeably with 'estrangement' (*Entfremdung*), makes a great deal more sense if derived from political economy than from philosophy. Admittedly, 'estrangement' figures in the earlier, philosophical writings quite often ('alienation', though, much more rarely), and also it could not be denied that there is a definite *sense* in which Marx's 'estrangement' is a *transposition* from the Feuerbachian critique of religion and idealist philosophy – in the *Manuscripts*, by the way, Marx does hold on to a number of Feuerbachian terms and notions, including the essential definition of humans as 'species-beings'. (Whether or not Feuerbach's, or Marx's, notion of alienation-estrangement has anything *validly* to do with Hegelian philosophy, its putative immediate 'parent', is a moot point but it need not concern us right here.) At any rate, Marx's 'alienation' (I will stick to this term right through) does show *continuity* with Left Hegelianism; it does have the meaning – which was the meaning of 'God' for Feuerbach – of the creature, the product assuming domination over the creator. In worshipping *things* or *ideas* we are really subjecting ourselves to the 'alien' rule of our own essential selves, our own species-nature acting *independently* of our conscious volition and proper interests. So far so good. But 'alienation' in the *Manuscripts* is not just a much enriched notion – compared to 'estrangement' in the 'Critique' and 'On the Jewish Question' – but is given, as it were, a robustly *objective* and *mundane* leg to stand on. No less an authority than Georg Lukacs advanced the suggestion in *The Young Hegel* that Marx actually translates the *English* term 'alienation' into the German '*Entaüsserung*' for the purposes of his unfolding argument in the *Manuscripts*. This English term is of course a part of the technical vocabulary of the science of political economy, employed by Smith, Ferguson and Steuart (as Marx himself remarks in the *Grundrisse* and *Theories of Surplus Value*). The meaning of 'alienation' in political economy is the simple, everyday, pedestrian *act of selling*. This meaning, I would suggest, is the *central* one in Marx's *Manuscripts*, notwithstanding the heady philosophical penumbra surrounding it.

The first substantive point to grasp about Marx's 'alienation' therefore is that its primary and chief reference is to an objective condition, or a material process, and not to a subjective feeling or 'state of consciousness'. This is just as well to keep in mind, for subsequently the *fashionable* understanding of the term – in radical sociology, existentialist philosophy, liberation theology for example – has become fastened on the subjective aspect, alienation being equated with such things as misery, loneliness, powerlessness, anomie, maladjustment and the like. It is true of course that this fashion has grown up to a considerable extent nurtured on the fashion of 'humanist' Marxism, and it is also true that the subjective aspect is a *part* of Marx's original meaning. But Marx is no more responsible for the sentimentalities of humanist Marxism than for the Stalinist purges – or perhaps he is responsible for both, what does it matter anyway. It does matter, however, quite a great deal that we see clearly *which way* Marx argues in the *Manuscripts*, and there is little doubt that he argues from the objective to the subjective, from a material process to a state of consciousness. And the second important point to grasp about Marx's alienation is that it therefore itself constitutes a 'mini-synthesis' as indeed being not just an aspect but the *innermost core* of his grand synthesis of revolution, political economy, and humanism. Alienation welds together, inseparably joins the religious 'estrangement' of humanism, the conflict, oppression and inequality stressed by revolutionary communist theory, and the exploitation, enslavement of labour as highlighted in the writings of the political economists. Alienation has then this treble root meaning in Marx's *Manuscripts*: it means that in the act of *selling* his productive capacity or 'labour power' (as the later technical refinement in the Marxist text will have it) the *worker* becomes *dominated* by that which he has thus sold. Everything else follows from this. It is in this 'treble equation' that we find the key to an understanding of the *whole* of Marxism.

The *Manuscripts* logically starts out from what Marx considers the fundamental 'contradiction' of the science of political economy. 'Labour' is said to produce all the wealth of modern society, yet labour is excluded from the enjoyment of this wealth. Marx also notes, pointedly, that by recognizing this basic contradiction in society political economy has gained the status of a proper science. But how to solve this contradiction? Marx's way, following the lead of the political economists, is to concentrate on and analyse 'labour' itself, as the creator of all social wealth. Marx here engages in a 'philosophical' definition of labour as essential human species-activity. Note that although Marx operates with the notion of 'species-being' adopted from Feuerbach, he puts all the emphasis on the practical, worldly aspect of human character. Man for Marx, as for Feuerbach, is a 'species-being' in that he identifies with the whole race, sees himself as a member and therefore as free and universal. But Marx here stresses that the ground for this 'subjective' aspect of species character is the distinctively human species-activity, labouring. It is this alone, in the last resort, which marks the human species off from the rest of nature. Animals are immediately identical with their activity; with humans their life-activity is a projection of themselves, it is their conscious aim. In other words, human action is inherently rational, and conversely human reason is inherently active, practical. (There is an emphatic restatement of Marx's view in *Capital*, in that famous passage about men and spiders and bees in the first volume.) It can be seen thus that what we described in broad terms in the first lecture as a central feature of the perspective of transcendence in European thought is concretely the very *starting-point* of Marxist thought. For Marx the human species is *unique* in the whole natural universe, and its transcendence is expressed by and attained through *labour*. It is just as well to note, of course, that this 'philosophical' notion of labour in the *Manuscripts* is an exceedingly complex one which it would be quite impossible to analyse here adequately. As commentators have noted, it contains an element of artistic creation, a religious residue, a philosophical resonance, as well as the reference to mundane sweat-and-toil. It is clear that Marx's notion of labour is closely modelled on Hegel's 'spirit', inheriting its character of primordial creativity; labour is the Demiurge, it is the Alpha and Omega of human life and society, the ultimate determinant of consciousness, *the* link between humanity and ultimate reality, and indeed it *makes* ultimate reality as far as humans are concerned. Marx himself in the *Manuscripts* (in a section which alas we shall have to ignore here) asserts that Hegel's spirit is in truth nothing but human labour clad in metaphysical garb. The validity of this assertion is somewhat doubtful but let us leave it at that.

Marx's main point though is that labour in its merely 'existential' aspects, in the actual conditions of modern society, does *not* come forth as human essential species-activity. It is the very opposite. The basic definition of modern society is precisely that in it labour is *alienated* – or to put it more pointedly the modern world is the world *of* alienated labour. Marx here first lists the dimensions of labour's alienation, and again it is important to note the sequence and relative emphasis. In the first instance – this being the basic dimension – labour is alienated from its life-giving raw material and its material product, i.e. from *nature*. The human being is for Marx objectively 'natural', a part of nature. This means dependence on nature in two ways. Nature is man's *body* which requires and receives constant material sustenance. And nature is also man's *soul*, in a manner of speaking, in that it alone provides the foil, the object for man's self-realization or humanization in labouring activity. (It is this second kind of dependence on nature which is missing with animals.) Labour is essentially 'objectification', i.e. the transformation of creative energy into products. In modern society, however, objectification is equivalent to alienation: those who 'labour' are separated from their own soul, as it were, at two points, at the beginning and at the end. They work on alien material and the product does not belong to them either. What remains is their sheer 'activity', exertion in between, and of course in these conditions labouring activity is also to be defined as alien activity, it is not undertaken for itself but 'sold' for a price, for something that is external to it. Marx very graphically uses the example of prostitution to explain what alienation means for labour: in both, that which should be the *end* is reduced to a mere *means*, and the external is elevated to a position of centrality.

It is only now that we come to the social, subjective and as it were psychological dimensions of alienation. They all follow from the alienation of labour from nature. It is because human beings have a false and inhuman relation to nature that their social affairs and consciousness also become twisted, the opposite of what they should be. Alienation from nature – i.e. the failure to objectify labour in nature in the proper human way – means of course dehumanization, subjection to the 'product', in a sense the *intrusion* of untamed nature into human affairs. A point with retrospective reference to some remarks made in our second lecture, on the 'gestation' of Marxism, should be made here: in 1844 the world of Adam Smith begins to assume predominance over the worlds of Rousseau and Hegel in Marx's scheme of ideas. What matters for Marx *primarily* is what men do to nature – or what they fail to do or what nature does to them – and *not* what they do to one another or to themselves. Nevertheless, there is enough limelight on the social dimension of alienation as well in the *Manuscripts*. Through alienation individuals become separated from the species and thus, on the surface and in their consciousness, lose their universality. Individual life, i.e. animal consumption, now becomes the end, and species-life, i.e. human production, becomes the means. Individuals are alienated from one another in the concrete: their essential relationship now is 'economic', i.e. *abstract*, external, egoistic, exploitative. And now on 'the other side', as Marx puts it, of the alienation of labour appear such phenomena as capital, the division of labour, the institution of private property, and a group or class of 'non-workers'. The text makes it absolutely clear that all these features of bourgeois capitalist class society are aspects *of* alienated labour and – in Marx's word – 'generated' out of the fundamental situation prevailing between nature and labour. There is therefore, if you like, a basic *materialist* principle coming to the fore already in the *Manuscripts*, albeit it is not the 'passive' and 'one-sided' materialism of the Enlightenment thinkers and Feuerbach (who receive criticism from Marx about the same time, in *The Holy Family* and the pithy 'Theses on Feuerbach' respectively), since, as we have seen, Marx's definition of labour *already* includes active human reason. Marx's thought (like Hegel's), it might be noted here, operates in terms of *relations*, not isolated abstract units, and hence his 'materialism' – as proclaimed of course more unambiguously in the later writings – is the assertion of the primacy of the labour–nature *relationship* over the labour–society relationship; Marxist materialism, in its basic original sense, means nothing more and nothing less.

Here, then, we have the rudiments of Marxism already laid out, visible. In human life, consciousness and society all that counts in the last resort is *labour*. Labour it is that defines, expresses and creates humanity. Labour it is that 'alienates' itself and thereby comes to *oppress itself*. Capital is nothing but labour in another form, labour as acting wildly, independently, like the broom of the sorcerer's apprentice. It is dominating, all-powerful, exploitative – but why? It is essential to grasp here the further point that the 'rule of capital' over labour is *possible* only because that which is alienated, that which is, vampire-like, sucking the blood of human beings, is *itself* labour, the essential and vital core of humanity. Nothing else would be capable of enslaving and exploiting human labour, since in the whole natural universe there is nothing higher, more potent than human labour! It is precisely because Marx sees labour as dynamic (creative, 'divine') that he can actually *derive* capital from it – thus supersede the standpoint of radical political economists before him; and it is because he correspondingly sees capital also as dynamic that he can *connect* the present to the future – thereby transcending the perspective of utopian socialism. Labour in movement created capital in the first place. Capital in movement is creating the conditions for its own supersession in future, nay, it is actively working *for* its own demise. Marx's 'science' of political economy (as elaborated by him later) is the science of *capital in movement*, and it is 'revolutionary' science in the precise and pointed sense that it's very subject matter is dynamic, revolutionary. The owners of capital or the class of 'non-workers', as presented in the *Manuscripts*, are simply the beneficiaries of the domination of capital, appendages to it, and their 'power' and their activity in 'exploiting' the labour of the working class are merely the visible emanation of the alienation of labour. *Human* activity alone counts, as we have said, and non-workers are strictly speaking sub-human, not because they are 'wicked' but because they are not engaged in the human process of labouring, i.e. not related *actively* to nature. As Marx says in the *Manuscripts*, non-workers are also 'alienated' but with them it is a passive state, not a direct result of their own activity. Thus we see the Marxist materialist and scientific standpoint visibly and dramatically surfacing out of the womb of philosophical humanism and communism, as fertilized by political economy. The concept of alienated labour is not, as such, Marxist revolutionary political economy, and the *Manuscripts* is certainly *no more* than jottings towards the eventual creation of *Capital*. But alienated labour *is* the fundamental principle of Marx's revolutionary social science, and therefore – on that level – we are entitled to say that Marx adds later nothing decisive to this core argument of the *Manuscripts*. With the *Manuscripts* Marxism is at last born; its genesis is over.

To round off the story of the *Manuscripts*, however, we should give a brief account of Marx's ideas concerning the future transcendence of the alienation of labour. This transcendence is that which bears the name, *communism*. It is possible, I think, to link these two concepts in the *Manuscripts* in a simple equation; alienation means the non-existence, absence of communism, and communism means nothing less and nothing more than the overcoming of alienation. Again, as with the alienation of labour and indeed following from it, we should note that Marx's concept of communism is synthetic also, in that it unites the human relation to nature, to society and internally to the mind. Communism is the realization of human species-character and hence it is the liberation, 'emancipation' of the human species in these three dimensions together. Communism is the transfiguration of humanity. In the *Manuscripts* Marx distinguishes between three stages or avenues pointing towards the attainment of this fully liberated state. Having dismissed various kinds of non-communist departures, like Proudhonism and utopian socialism, he identifies first a so-called 'crude communism' which consists in the 'generalization', rather than the abolition, of private property, i.e. its *external* abolition only, while retaining its 'spirit' and consciousness. Crude communism means levelling down, it is the apotheosis of greed, envy, avarice, the *simple* opposition to capitalism, a mere reflection of the 'unnatural' crudeness of workers nurtured in capitalist society. (In the previous lecture we already referred to the connection between Marx's 'crude communism' and the perspective of the early revolutionary communists.) Then comes an intermediary stage of which Marx says very little and what he does say is somewhat arcane. Perhaps we need not worry about it though. And the crowning stage is 'full communism', the 'positive transcendence' of private property (i.e. external as well as internal), the *genuine resolution* of all maladies, contradictions, tribulations at present afflicting human beings. The heady peroration on communism as 'genuine resolution' in the *Manuscripts* is well known, indeed bandied about in all commentaries on the early Marx, so I shall resist the temptation of quoting it in full.

Communism is liberation in three dimensions. It is the conscious assertion of human 'divinity' in the realm of morals, the final confirmation and proof of man's independence in the universe. Communism is 'practical atheism', not the abstract denial of the existence of God but the actual *experience* of acting freely in nature and society, the experience of human self-creation in labour. Secondly, communism is the union of the human species with nature, the development of a new kind of 'human nature'. Whereas in their present degraded, dehumanized state human beings relate to nature and to themselves only 'abstractly', as objects to be used, in communism this relationship will be full and 'concrete'. There will be a conscious *need* to develop individual potentialities to the full and to participate in and identify with the whole range of human activities, superseding the acquisitive urge. In communism we shall 'have' nothing but we shall *be* everything. (I cannot resist, however, one digressive and rueful remark here: only a twenty-six-year-old could seriously advance ideas like this!) Natural objects will be experienced directly, through artistic appreciation and enjoyment. The human 'senses' will become 'theoreticians' and integrated; there will be no divorce between thinking and being, passions and the brain. Science will be united with industry and there will be only one science, the science of man as natural and of nature as human. (Again, it could just be noted in passing that – as a number of commentators have noted – in the section on communism in the *Manuscripts* Marx sometimes veers dangerously close to a position that could be construed as a kind of philosophical 'idealism'. Be that as it may, I don't think that this affects the basic 'materialism' – as explained above – of Marx's labour-oriented *social* perspective.) And thirdly, communism signifies the unity of the species, the abolition of the contradiction between 'individual' and 'society'. This means, as Marx stresses, no imposition of an abstract social whole over individual personality (*à la* Rousseau and the revolutionary communists?) but the full conscious recognition – and again, actual *experience* – of the universal, inherently 'social' species-nature of individuals. Just as there will be in communism a human 'need' to experience nature and all human activities directly, so there will also be a 'need' to identify and act in harmony with one's fellows in society. So it's all sweet and honey, in nature, in society, and in consciousness. *Heaven is on earth.* Communism is the grand conclusion of the modern convergence of the two perspectives of transcendence and understanding in the European tradition.

Finally it might be observed that the *Manuscripts* contains two alternative – though not necessarily incompatible – models or visions of communist relationship in this bright future. One is based on the relationship of sex. This beautiful passage from the *Manuscripts* must be quoted:

> The direct, natural and necessary relation of person to person is the relation of man to woman. In this natural relation of the sexes man's relation to nature is immediately his relation to man, just as his relation to man is immediately his relation to nature – his own natural function. In this relationship, therefore is sensuously manifested, reduced to an observable fact, the extent to which the human essence has become nature to man, or to which nature has to him become the human essence of man . . . In this relationship is revealed, too, the extent to which, therefore, the other person as a person has become for him a need – the extent to which he in his individual existence is at the same time a social being.

It would be difficult to improve on this concise, and definitely inspired, description of a basic relationship which is indeed palpably the *synthesis* of the 'human' and the 'natural'. For one thing – and we remarked on this in passing earlier, in connection with Fourier – passages of this kind would very categorically divide Marx off from latter-day 'sexual radicalism'. Even if Marx's vision of full communism is sex-based – as has been alleged – it is to be noted that sex for him (and for Engels) is essentially a *relationship*, the union of the 'personal' and the 'natural', and not a means of instinctual *gratification*, i.e. the 'natural' *arrested* on the abstract individual level. But it is by no means certain that the sex-relationship is *that* basic to Marx's communist vision. Another purple passage in the *Manuscripts* extols the experience of comradeship among workers:

> Such things as smoking, drinking, eating, etc. are no longer means of contact or means that bring together. Company, association and conversation, which again has society as its end, are enough for them; the brotherhood of man is no mere phrase with them, but a fact of life, and the

nobility of man shines upon us from their work-hardened bodies.

As I suggested, the two models or projections are by no means incompatible. Communism in the image of the bedroom and communism in the image of the pub are equally thrilling scenarios to contemplate and even better in combination. In a more serious vein, however, and in the light of what seems to me to be the overall thrust of the *Manuscripts* – signalling the further development of Marx's thought – the relationship of 'comradeship' should probably be assigned primacy over the sex-relationship. Sexuality after all, even in Marx's naturalized terms, is as it were an inward-looking engagement on the part of the species, an expression of *species-egoism*, nothing but generalized 'consumption' on a gigantic scale. Sex has, as such, nothing *productively* to do with nature outside. If we do accept, as I think reading the *Manuscripts* we should, that in and for Marxism the primary definition and programmatic task for the human race is the struggle with nature – the foe who is met through *labour* – then it seems to follow that fellowship defined in terms of this struggle is the 'human' fellowship *par excellence*. And this of course connotes in the first instance the relationship of 'class', and in particular the class of the proletariat, and through the proletariat humanity itself as perpetually active, perpetually self-transcendent, reaching for the stars.

*   *   *

What remains, then, is for us briefly to pull the threads together and wind up these four lectures on the genesis of Marxism. It is somewhat banal to make the point that Marx's career as a writer and public figure only *begins* in earnest after the *Manuscripts*. Marxism may have been 'born' in Paris in 1844 but the trajectory of its growing years was taking it far afield, together with Marx's own peregrinations. In 1845 Marx moved to Brussels, getting deeply involved in communist organization and correspondence, and thence a short time later to London which became his domicile for the rest of his life, interrupted only occasionally, the most notable instance being his participation in revolutionary events in Paris and Cologne in 1848. The development of Marx's doctrine, as we have already suggested, followed *more or less* the direction of his geographical moves and was influenced also by the secular events of nineteenth-century European and world history. The concept of 'alienated labour', however, remained the foundation stone of the whole impressive intellectual building of Marxism erected after 1844. It may be useful here to distinguish between three subsequent 'storeys' resting on the foundations of the *Manuscripts*. In the first place Marx's 'materialist conception of history' gains its formulation in the vast manuscript pages of *The German Ideology* (1845), and as published in Marx's lifetime in *The Poverty of Philosophy* (1847), the *Communist Manifesto* (1848), and in the most succinct presentation in the famous Preface to *A Contribution to the Critique of Political Economy* (1859). Though in many ways this is a simplification, it could still be suggested that Marxist historical materialism is no more really than a *systematization* of the story of the alienation of labour and its transcendence. The 'materialism' of this historical doctrine lies precisely in the elevation of the human relationship to nature ('mode of production') over the human relationship in society, and the decisive move in that direction is of course already encountered in the *Manuscripts*.

Marx's theory of politics, revolution, class and class struggle, matures around the mid-century, in the atmosphere of heady expectations and bitter disappointments. Apart from the *Manifesto*, Marx's 'Address to the Central Committee of the Communist League' (1850) and above all the brilliant piece, *The Eighteenth Brumaire of Louis Bonaparte* (1851) – arguably, together with 'On the Jewish Question', the most delectable piece of Marxist writing for *non-Marxist* students of European political and social theory – stand testimony to Marx's political acumen, his powers of observation and analysis, his skill in connecting high theory with practical strategy and tactics. And then finally Marx's work culminates in his theory of capitalist production, as set out – again in a thrilling fashion – in the manuscript pages of the *Grundrisse*, the three grand volumes of *Capital* and the three heavy tomes of *Theories of Surplus Value*. Again, perhaps it is not too much of an exaggeration to say that the Marxist theory of surplus value and exploitation *directly*, and Marx's 'macro-economic' theory of capitalist development (crises, global spread, finance capital, the falling rate of profit, etc.) *indirectly*, grow out of the basic insight of the *Manuscripts*, fastening on the dynamic nature of capital as 'alienated labour'. I would like to make the same point here as was advanced at the very beginning of these lectures, in connection with the relation of Marxist thought to the mainstream European tradition of political and social theory in general. European thought need not have produced anything like Marxism. But only European thought *could* have produced Marxism. Similarly, the standpoint of Marx's *Manuscripts* need not have led to the production of *Capital*. But it is the standpoint of the *Manuscripts* which can alone make the scientific categories and run of arguments in *Capital* fully intelligible. In endeavouring to account for the genesis of Marxism one need not go further than this, I hope.

Marx's later work – books, articles, reviews, a vast correspondence, and further manuscript notes – extends in many directions, and perhaps I need not stress that the above categorization into three larger clusters of theory is not exhaustive. But, in justification of organizing the story of the genesis of Marx's thought in the way it has been done here, I would like to add two further points briefly. Firstly, the assumption on which these lectures were compiled is that there is such a thing as 'Marxism', in the singular, i.e. that Marx's thought has some sort of underlying unity, a heart, a distinctive thread, a hard inner core (whatever metaphor we are using). I obviously think that there is such a unity, that it is of interest to locate it, and that it does lie in the concept of alienated labour in the *Manuscripts*, the tangible expression of Marxism as synthesis. It is certainly permissible – though it may not be so *interesting* – to study Marx on the assumption that his views had no such underlying unity but that – as the case may be – one or another of his researches, investigations, theories, etc. are of particular interest to scholars working in various fields or political activists intent on pursuing sundry goals. If this is the case, then of course the *Manuscripts* will not necessarily be seen to occupy a special position in the corpus. I do not wish to judge this eclectic tendency in Marx-scholarship, except to repeat that such a 'dissolution' of Marxism takes a great deal of the fun out of studying Marxism and (more seriously) ultimately leads away from such a study altogether. Directly opposed to this *eclectic* tendency there is another which may be called the *dogmatic* tendency (this being my second point) which does assume the unity of Marxism to be unbroken and the hard core doctrine to be entirely valid – indeed the *only* valid teaching in political and social theory extant today. On this reading, too, the central importance of the *Manuscripts* might well be denied, and instead the *Manifesto* and/or *Capital* (usually) placed on the pedestal. But to me it appears clearer than daylight that it is only staunchly believing and 'practising' Marxists who would take a serious interest in a so-called 'epistemological break' in Marx's thought after 1844, or in Marx's practical strategy concerning the arousal of revolutionary class consciousness, or in the technical details of Marx's theory of exploitation. I have respect for such a stance, though I do not share it. However, the point I am trying to make here is that no one could really be a believing and practising Marxist unless such a person accepted the validity of the concept of alienated labour as formulated in the *Manuscripts*. The latter is implicit in mature Marxism. Therefore in the last analysis it is a question of either swallowing Marxism 'dogmatically' or – which is the path chosen here – attempting to go back to its roots and making its implicit core visible. Marxist belief and practice *may* follow from such an undertaking but they need not.

To go back then to our story: the genesis of Marxism has been presented here as the synthesis of elements, traditions, departures found in the history of Western culture. We have looked at Marx's synthesis on two levels. On the deeper level – or if you like in a more extensive historical context – I have argued that Marx's thought unites the two underlying perspectives of European thought, the perspective of religious or idealistic transcendence and the perspective of scientific or materialistic understanding. Alienation and its overcoming in communism can be taken to stand for 'understanding' and 'transcendence' respectively, and of course in Marxism these two categories are inseparably linked, indeed interpenetrating. Marxism contends that the way to transcend actual existence lies exclusively through a thorough understanding of actual existence, and conversely that the proper understanding of this world is achieved by fastening on that which it is not, on its 'negation', i.e. on the transcendent itself. On the more immediate level – or in a narrower historical context – we have presented Marx's thought as the synthesis of three modern departures (which follows an interpretation of Marxism more commonly encountered in the literature). Here the bottom layer, as it were, was identified as classical European liberalism, with its different crystallizations in politics, society and philosophy. On top of that we have located Marx's immediate intellectual background, respectively in the three departures of revolutionary communism, utopian socialism, and radical humanism. These two large contexts, I have endeavoured to argue, are themselves to be seen as interpenetrating. The three modern departures named issue out of the *modern* 'synthesis' of understanding and transcendence; they all assert, in their different ways, that the 'good society' is attainable, and that it is attainable through knowledge, understanding. In the first lecture I indicated also that there may be some problems attaching to the very root ideas involved in the two underlying perspectives, as bequeathed to the three modern departures and finally to Marxism.

Marx's thought centres on human liberation, in the three areas of nature, society and the human mind. These respectively go back to the modern science of political economy, the revolutionary communist view of social conflict and its resolution, and humanist philosophy, all three of which Marx adapted from the teachings of his predecessors and contemporaries. Earlier in this lecture I ventured a few remarks concerning the significance of the 'accidental' sequence in which these three departures came to be absorbed into Marxism. Having traced the story of Marx's intellectual development to what I have called the 'birth' of Marxism in the *Manuscripts*, I would now like to continue and conclude on this particular topic. Marx *consummated* – and this is definitely the right word – his intellectual career by becoming a social scientist or political economist; indeed he more or less invented the *revolutionary science* of political economy. The main principle or conceptual starting-point of this revolutionary science is 'alienated labour' which Marx defines in the *Manuscripts* for the first time. I have emphasized that in the context of Marx's development up to this point – and of course with far-reaching significance in the light of the further elaboration of his doctrine – this marks the enthrone-ment of a *materialist* major premise in his scheme of ideas. This must mean, in terms of Marx's three-pronged doctrine of human liberation, the assertion of the primacy of *liberation in nature*. I would therefore suggest that we define the final and core 'message' contained in Marxism in this concise statement, and never mind the rhetoric: solve the problem of the human relationship to nature, and the rest will follow! That is to say, once we *know* how to deal with, contain and thus 'conquer' nature, and are in our actual *practice* adequate to this task, then and not before we can attain liberty in society and can also finally banish the crippling superstitions of the human mind, all lingering fetishisms, reifications, religious and metaphysical residues. Everything leads back to *nature*, the ultimate reality, including ultimate human reality, and to human *labour* which is our special species-link to it. In the distinctive 'scientific' language of Marxism, as it matured after 1844, the message is of course formulated in terms of the causal primacy of the 'mode of production': production, labour advances first, then come corresponding changes in the political and social structure, and the transformation of consciousness. The triumph of labour in nature brings about communism in society, and communism heralds in human freedom and happiness.

Can or should we then address ourselves to the simplest but also most important question of all, namely was Marx right or wrong in proclaiming this message? In a way, of course, one can never tell: like religious prophecies of either doom or salvation, the Marxist message in its deepest essence is his-torically open-ended: it may always happen *tomorrow* that advances in production will achieve the extent of 'liberation' in the man-nature relationship necessary to overcome alienation, oppression and exploitation in society, and thereafter it's Bob's your uncle. What we can say, however – with due modesty and circumspection, although the point is commonplace enough – is that this liberation has not quite come about so far. 'Marxism in the world' has greatly prospered, no doubt, but not I think in the manner originally envisaged by its founder. Instead of 'changing the world' (which Marx himself named as the *crucial* thing in the 'Theses on Feuerbach'), it has itself become a part of the world, a part of 'actual existence'. Curiously the subsequent development of Marxism has shown a *reverse* of Marx's own intellectual journey, culminating in what we have presented as the final message. This message has in time become more and more diluted, devolved and (what must be seen) in Marxist terms *retrogressive*. Marx himself journeyed from philosophy through politics to his own social science – from the mind to society and then to economy – from moralizing through politicizing to the final certainty of his theory of capital. Marxism it seems has undergone a process of journeying in the exactly opposite direction: starting as superior and unified *science* (in the great era of the Second International), it has become self-standing *politics* (in Marxism-Leninism and its various offshoots), and finally it has reverted to being *philosophy* (most importantly in so-called 'Western Marxism'), i.e. a highly respected, influential and sophisticated 'academic' perspective, represented in all branches of learning and culture, almost a kind of 'conventional wisdom' in extensive circles, with a lot to *say* but relatively little to *do*. Within the area of Marxist 'politics' in the narrower sense, reversing in all fronts is also noticeable, not to say conspicuous: see for instance the historic compromises with nationalism, statism, legalism, organized religion and even the market. The truth is (and of course this is a greatly simplified, though I hope not unduly distorted picture) that the extensive and intensive growth of Marxism has been accompanied by its global presentation of what amounts to a *defensive posture*.

And as well as noting the slow retreat of Marxism in the face of a recalcitrant, obstinate world of 'actual existence', signifying a global conservative counter-attack on Marxist radicalism, we must also note here the successive waves of assaults on the 'Left flank' of Marxism, presenting the onward march of radical thought and movements. It is not just that Marxism has not proven to be the 'word' for everybody, left, right and centre; it has not even been the 'last word' on the radical side. Freud, Nietzsche, Foucault and a dozen or so other luminaries in the radical firmament have since the last century, if not exactly 'dwarfed' Marx, certainly put him 'in his place'. The great contemporary issues, for example, of cultural equality and co-existence, and feminine liberation, do reach essentially *beyond* Marxism, though of course earnest efforts are being made all the time to incorporate them into Marxism, to 'up-date' Marxism in these and other areas. There is a suspicion though – and it is by no means my suspicion alone – that this process of extension, just like the process of internal 'dilution' referred to in the previous paragraph, will have to come to an end at some point. Marxism as a doctrine will become well-nigh *meaningless* and *pointless* if it continues with the attempt to subsume everything under its banner, market-individualism on the Right and simultaneously (or alternatively) anti-sexism and multi-culturalism on the Left. The old bottle can take so much but no more. All in all, the opinion might be ventured here that the overall message of Marx has now been recognized for its inadequacy: whatever the key to a proper understanding of human life, consciousness, society and politics might be, and whichever way we should seek happiness and liberation, these are not *just* to be sought in the alienation of labour and its overcoming in communism.

So then, finally, we ought to restate the view with which these lectures on the genesis of Marxism started out. The *interest* of Marxism and the *value* of Marxism lie very squarely with its place in the whole tradition of European culture and civilization. Marxism took up, and vitally redefined, the traditional Western concepts and values of reason, freedom, historical movement, criticism and the characteristic view of the human species as unique in nature. All these notions and values are being redefined constantly, and the process has been going on *since* Marx. But in fact the on-going supersession of Marxism is the greatest accolade one can pay to Marxism. It is itself a confirmation of the place of Marxism in the mainstream. The 'genesis' of Marxism, as I attempted to adumbrate in the foregoing pages, is now perhaps seen more clearly and emphatically as the story of a very important *chapter*, no more and no less, in the history of Western political and social theory. Marxism has not appeared out of an empty vacuum and it has not issued in a cul-de-sac. Marx left his mark. The story after the genesis of Marxism must be one in the genesis of which Marxism *itself* counts as an element.

SELECT BIBLIOGRAPHY

Acton, H. B., *The Illusion of the Epoch: Marxism–Leninism as a Philosophical Creed*, London, Cohen and West, 1955

Arthur, C. J., *Dialectics of Labour*, Oxford, Blackwell, 1986

Avineri, S., *The Social and Political Thought of Karl Marx*, Cambridge, CUP, 1968

—— *Hegel's Theory of the Modern State*, Cambridge, CUP, 1972

—— *Moses Hess: Prophet of Communism and Zionism*, New York, New York University Press, 1985

Berki, R. N., *Insight and Vision: the Problem of Communism in Marx's Thought*, London, Dent, 1983

Blaug, M., *Ricardian Economics: an Historical Study*, New Haven, Yale University Press, 1958

Bray, J. F. *Labour's Wrongs and Labour's Remedy* (1839), London, LSE, 1931

Buonarotti, P., *Babeuf's Conspiracy for Equality*, New York, A. M. Kelly, 1965

Carver, T., *Marx's Social Theory*, Oxford, OUP, 1982

Cole, G. D. H., *A History of Socialist Thought*, vol. i, London, Macmillan, 1953

Dupre, L., *The Philosophical Foundations of Marxism*, New York, Harcourt, Brace and World, 1966

Durkheim, E., *Socialism and Saint-Simon*, London, Routledge and Kegan Paul, 1959

Evans, M., *Karl Marx*, London, Allen and Unwin, 1975

Feuerbach, L. A., *The Essence of Christianity* (1841), New York, Harper and Row, 1957

Fishman, W. J., *The Insurrectionists*, London, Methuen, 1970

Fried, A. and Sanders, R., eds., *A Documentary History of Socialist Thought*, Edinburgh, The University Press, 1964

Fromm, L., *Marx's Concept of Man*, New York, Ungar, 1961

Fourier, C., *The Utopian Vision* (Selected Texts, trans. and intro. by J. Beecher and R. Bienvenu), London, Cape, 1971

Geoghegan, V., *Utopianism and Marxism*, London, Methuen, 1987

Goodwin, B. and Taylor, K., *The Politics of Utopia: a Study in Theory and Practice*, London, Hutchinson, 1982

171

Gray, A., *The Socialist Tradition: Moses to Lenin*, London, Longmans, 1946

Hegel, G. W. F., *The Phenomenology of Spirit* (1807), trans. by A. V. Miller, Oxford, Clarendon, 1977

——— *The Philosophy of Right* (1821), trans. by T. M. Knox, Oxford, Clarendon, 1962

Hodgskin, T., *Labour Defended against the Claims of Capital* (1825), London, Hammersmith Reprints, 1964

Hook, S., *From Hegel to Marx*, New York, The Humanities Press, 1958

Kamenka, E., *The Ethical Foundations of Marxism*, London, Routledge and Kegan Paul, 1972

Kolakowski, L., *Main Currents of Marxism*, vol. i, Oxford, Clarendon, 1978

Leeuwen, A. van, *Critique of Heaven*, London, Lutterworth Press, 1972

Lichtheim, G., *The Origins of Socialism*, London, Weidenfeld and Nicolson, 1969

Lindgren, J. R., *The Social Philosophy of Adam Smith*, The Hague, Nijhoff, 1973.

Lukacs, G., *The Young Hegel*, London, Merlin Press, 1975

MacGregor, D., *The Communist Ideal in Hegel and Marx*, London, Allen and Unwin, 1984

McLellan, D., *Karl Marx: his Life and Thought*, London, Macmillan, 1973

——— *Marx before Marxism*, London, Macmillan, 1970

——— *The Young Hegelians and Karl Marx*, London, Macmillan, 1969

——— *Marxism and Religion*, London, Macmillan, 1987

Maguire, J. M. *Marx's Paris Writings: an Analysis*, Dublin, Gill and Macmillan, 1972

Manuel, F. E. *The New World of Henri Saint-Simon*, Cambridge, Mass., Harvard University Press, 1956.

Marcuse, H. *Reason and Revolution: Hegel and the Rise of Social Theory*, London, Routledge, 1968

Marx, K. and Engels, F., *Collected Works*, vols. i and iii, London, Lawrence and Wishart, 1975

Meszaros, I., *Marx's Theory of Alienation*, London, Merlin Press, 1970

Miranda, J. P., *Marx against the Marxists: the Christian Humanism of Karl Marx*, London, SCM Press, 1980

Ollman, B., *Alienation; Marx's Conception of Man in Capitalist Society*, Cambridge, CUP, 1971

Owen, R., *A New View of Society* (1814), Harmondsworth, Pelican Books, 1970

Parekh, B., *Marx's Theory of Ideology*, London, Croom Helm, 1981

Pelczynski, Z. A., ed., *Hegel's Political Philosophy*, Cambridge, CUP, 1971

——— *The State and Civil Society*, Cambridge CUP, 1984

Plant, R., *Hegel*, London, Allen and Unwin, 1973

Riedel, M., *Between Tradition and Revolution: the Hegelian Transformation of Political Philosophy*, Cambridge, CUP, 1984

Rigby, S.H., *Marxism and History*, Manchester, The University Press, 1987

Ritter, J., *Hegel and the French Revolution*, Cambridge, Mass., MTI Press, 1982

Rousseau, J.-J., *Discourse on the Origins of Inequality* (1755), London, Dent, 1963

Saint-Simon, H., *Political Thought* (ed. by G. Ionescu) Oxford, OUP, 1976

—— *Selected Writings* (ed. by F.M.H. Markham), Oxford, Blackwell, 1952

Salvadori, M., ed., *Modern Socialism*, London, Macmillan, 1968

Scott, J.A. ed., *The Defence of Gracchus Babeuf*, Cambridge, Mass., University of Massachusetts, 1967

Sherover-Marcuse, E., *Emancipation and Consciousness*, Oxford, Blackwell, 1986

Smith, A., *An Inquiry into the Nature and Causes of the Wealth of Nations* (1776), Harmondsworth, Pelican Books, 1970

Spitzer, A.B., *The Revolutionary Theories of August Blanqui*, New York, Columbia University Press, 1957

Stepelevich, L.S., ed., *The Young Hegelians*, Cambridge, CUP, 1983

Talmon, J.L. *The Origins of Totalitarian Democracy*, New York, Praeger, 1961

Taylor, C., *Hegel*, Cambridge, CUP, 1975

Taylor, K., *The Political Thought of the Utopian Socialists*, London, Cass, 1982

Tholfsen, R.R., *Ideology and Revolution in Modern Europe*, New York, Columbia University Press, 1984

Thompson, N.W., *The People's Science*, Cambridge, CUP, 1984

Tucker, R.C., *Philosophy and Myth in Karl Marx*, Cambridge, CUP, 1961

Wartofsky, M.W., *Feuerbach*, Cambridge, CUP, 1977

Wolfson, M., *Marx: Economist, Philosopher, Jew: Steps in the Development of a Doctrine*, London, Macmillan, 1982

INDEX OF NAMES